The Lean Business System Cultural Building Blocks

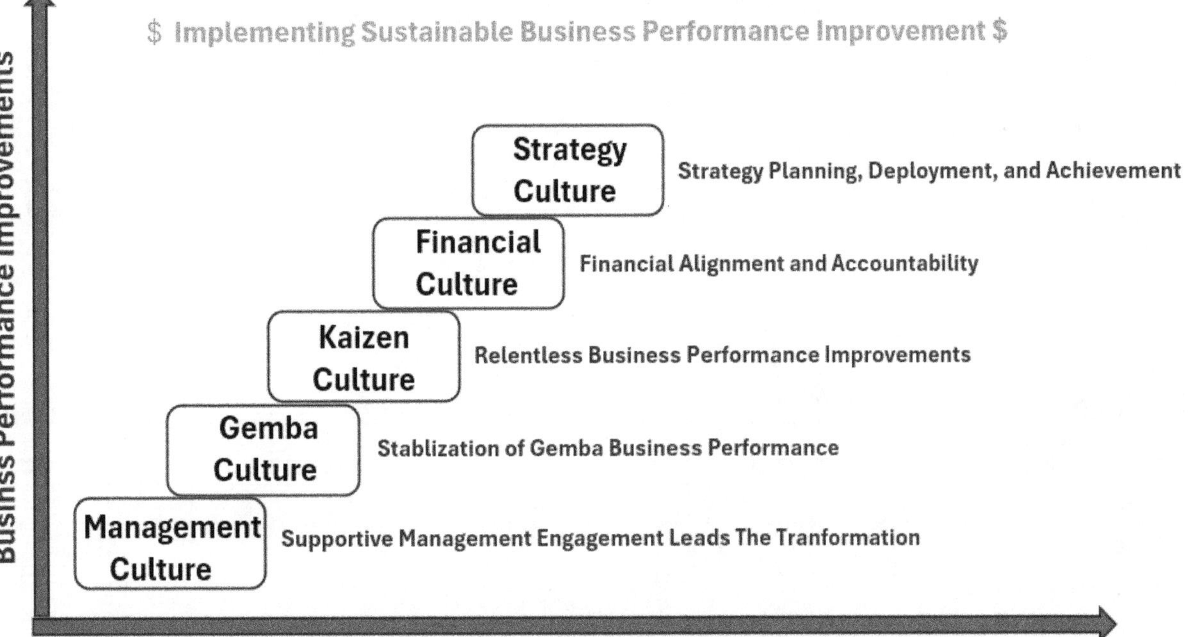

A Practical Guide to Creating (or Improving) A Lean Business System.

By David Michael Sparks

"Continuous Improvement is Better Than Delayed Perfection."

Mark Twain

TABLE OF CONTENTS

INTRODUCTION

To begin, this is not an AI generated publication. There are literally thousands of Lean Manufacturing and Lean Business System internet posts and articles that provide AI generated overviews and "snippets" of Lean Manufacturing and Six Sigma tools to spark interest among practitioners and non-practitioners alike. While many of these elementary Lean and Six Sigma snippets are good advertising for the companies or individuals that publish them, many of them are painfully repetitive, out of context, and incorrectly sequenced for building a complete Lean Business System. A good example is the multiple postings about Takt Time as a Lean Tool. If not explained in the context of Design For Flow, Line Balancing, Continuous Flow, and Level Loading, the reader does not have complete information on how to optimally use the Takt Time tool. The reader only has a snippet of information. This is much like attempting to learn to play a musical instrument from watching YouTube video clips. While one may learn musical fragments, the practitioner may never entirely understand the subject of music theory. In musical terms, this may be called noodling, never reaching full potential. There is not much use for just noodling in the Business Arena, stakeholders are expecting optimal performance, results, and returns on investments.

Implementing snippets of Lean Methodology and/or Six Sigma Methodology may sound great and may even offer a temporary sense of unsustainable instant gratification when they are implemented. But implementing snippets of Lean Manufacturing and Six Sigma will not yield a complete and sustainable Lean Business System. In fact, a Lean Business System should not be thought of as only Lean Manufacturing. Methodologies such as Lean Manufacturing to eliminate waste and Six Sigma to reduce or eliminate variation are important contributors to the Lean Business System, but they are certainly not the whole Lean Business System.

An organization should be able to start the Lean Business System journey economically, depending on their current state Lean status and the desired velocity of implementation. To illustrate the point, refer the story below, based on a true manufacturing event.

A plant manager and his staff were being introduced to the Lean Manufacturing Methodology for the first time. The plant manager (let's call him Joe) leaned back in his chair and thought "What is this flavor of the month program now". But since Lean Methodology was a corporate mandate, he had no choice but to go along with the program. Fortunately for Joe, he had a very knowledgeable Lean Practitioner assigned to him that led the first Kaizen event in Joe's plant.

Upon completion of the event and the formal report out, Joe was impressed. He was even more impressed when he saw a real productivity gain on his Profit & Loss (Income Statement). After that first Kaizen event Joe became fully management engaged with Lean Methodology in his plant.

The point of this simple illustration is twofold:

- The plant did not spend hundreds of thousands of dollars to get started, although many may argue that Joe's plant should have started differently. But starting somewhere is better than waiting for "Delayed Perfection".
- Everything that is done on the manufacturing shop floor, or really anywhere in the business, does show up in the organization's financial Profit & Loss.

Managers and Lean practitioners must learn to read and understand the organization's Profit & Loss and be able to:

- Recognize financial waste. Understanding and analyzing the Profit & Loss is another method of seeing waste that is occurring in the organization.
- Understand the P&L, and learn to speak the "Financeze" language when conversing Lean Methodology with higher echelon management. Lean practitioners will argue that cost accounting and absorption based accounting practices are anti-lean. Whether true or not, standard accounting principles are probably here to stay, so Lean practitioners must learn to be successful within those measurements. Also, those who make this absorption based financial accounting argument are assuming that no other business measures or metrics exist to keep in check the perceived potential abuse of favorably inflating the Profit & Loss. That may be due to the fact that they really do not understand the Profit & Loss.

Financial Management is certainly a key contributor and stakeholder to Lean Methodology. Financial knowledge and consistent Financial Management engagement is paramount to the success of the Lean Business System.

The Lean Business System is much more than a conglomerate of Lean and Six Sigma Projects. It is the way associates, all associates, in the organization are culturally engaged to make the business continually better. The Lean Business System initiative starts with an organization's Vision to be Lean across all business disciplines. Strategic deployment and achievement planning to describe success, and the daily execution at every deployment phase in order to maintain the strategic deployment on schedule. Executed correctly, It becomes the cultural spine of the organization. In fact, it should become so engrained into the cultural DNA of the organization that it is invisible, and associates embrace it as a normal way of conducting business. It becomes the unspoken rule that if one cannot embrace the organization's Lean Business System Culture, then that personnel will not be an organizational fit. In fact, the aptitude to "fit the Lean culture" should be a key Human Resources selection criteria.

> "Culture change is probably the most absurd of all the ideas in the people management lexicon. People's behaviour is governed by the system, so when you change the system the culture changes, for free!"

The above quote was extracted from a LinkedIn ′snippet article′. The original misguided author is unknown.

THIS IS JUST NOT TRUE

"Manufacturing culture is characterized by the values, behaviors, and attitudes of the company's leadership and employees. A good company culture can positively impact employee engagement, retention, business success, and the bottom line".

Culture in any organization is critically important. Without culture, an organization is just a collection of equipment, personnel, policies, and procedures, all of which will go just so far, never reaching its true performance potential. Positive Engagement Culture is the electricity in the air that creates highly engaged-high performance associates that are motivated and capable of delivering continuous business improvements and discovering breakthrough innovations.

By learning and implementing the Lean Business System tools and cultures in an organized and systematic layered approach, these highly engaged-high performance associates will develop a sustainable foundation and capability to use the Lean Business System tools. This will produce a culture of improved associate engagement and satisfaction, providing incremental and exponentially increasing business performance improvements.

Executed correctly and consistently, the system evolves into a self-perpetual business improvement culture where relentless continuous improvement behavior is just the way business is done, by management and all associates. A cash machine that fosters Customer, Associate and Shareholder satisfaction. With the organization´s consistent management engagement and dedication, the continuous improvement culture will transition wider and deeper across all of the organization's business disciplines.

The Lean Business System Cultural Building Blocks for Success.

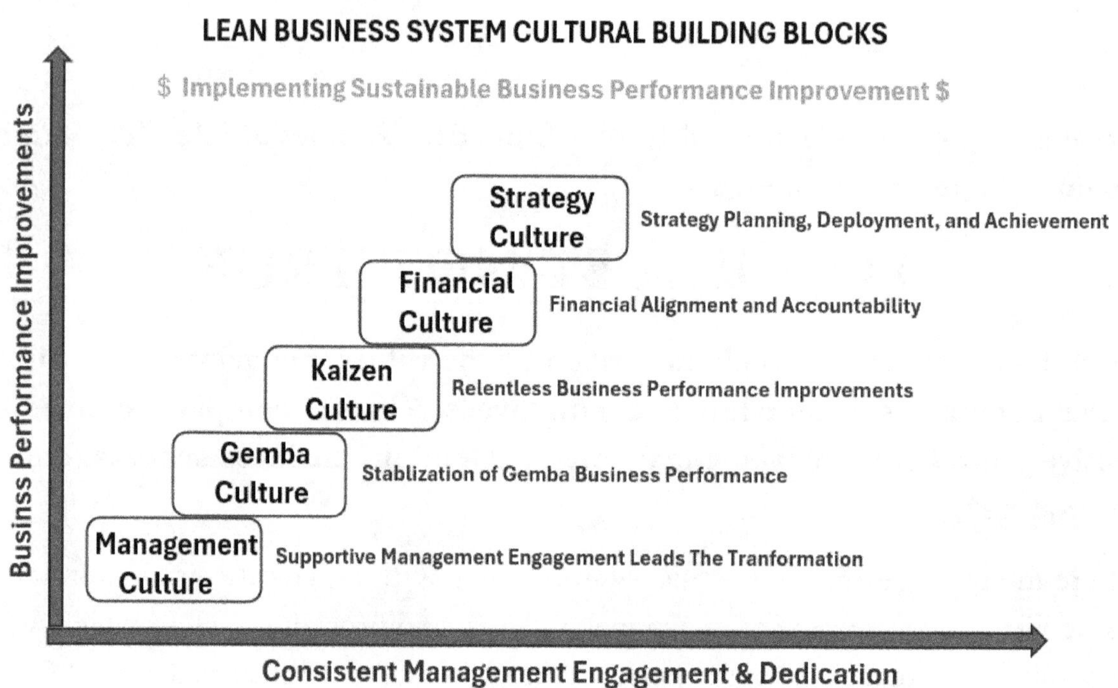

To accomplish this, a layered approach to the change of behaviors as shown above is recommended. An organization does not have to wait to finish one building block in order to start another, as is shown by the overlapping blocks illustration. In fact, they can and should be in pursuit of perfection in all building blocks phases, at all times to some degree. It is also critically important to not skip a block. Regarding the example of Joe's plant, Joe and his organization would have been much farther ahead had they at least had the knowledge contained in all five of the Lean Business System building blocks instead of starting in the middle of the Kaizen Tools and Culture block.

While it is important to pursue perfection in all building blocks, it is also important to understand that the Lean Business System does not function optimally with partial blocks. For example, Gemba does not function optimally if Management is not optimally engaged, and Kaizen does not function optimally is Gemba is not functioning optimally. Also, this is true regarding descending blocks. All the lower blocks will function more optimally if the above blocks are functioning optimally. All blocks do have a dependency upon each other, up and down the steps. But this should not hinder an organization from moving forward. They should not get caught up in the delayed perfection trap. By working all of the blocks consistently, the whole system will improve exponentially. One should think of management engagement as the cement that binds the Lean Business System building blocks together.

Managers that do not take seriously the topic of the Lean Business System tools and required cultural change should prepare themselves for a professional life of consistent mediocracy and constant business crisis management.

Enjoy The Journey...

*Several of the format illustrations in this publication are abbreviated to facilitate reduced page lengths.

UNIT 1 - MANAGEMENT TOOLS & CULTURE

Supportive Management Engagement Leads The Transformation.

"What is not important to Management,
will not be important to the rest of the organization"

The Foundation Step of the Lean Business System Building Blocks implementation is the Management Culture. Managers are the first to undergo cultural change and need to understand that their professional life is about to change for the better. But to realize this change for the better, managers will be required to transition from a traditional controlling organization hierarchy to an inverse supporting role hierarchy. This transition is to ensure that value add associates have all of the information, training, tools, and motivation required to manage their responsibility at Gemba.

The Lean Business System is a professional lifetime commitment. Unlike other initiatives or projects, this is not an initiative with a three month, or six month, or even a twelve month project timeline. It is a cultural change of the never ending pursuit of perfection. This change can be significant depending on the current state of management engagement and of the Lean maturity of an organization. The illustration below shows some management and organizational behaviors that will change as the organization turns the traditional organizational hierarchy triangle upside down, migrating toward the supportive Lean Business System management hierarchy. Consistent management engagement and support are required to accomplish this hierarchy change.

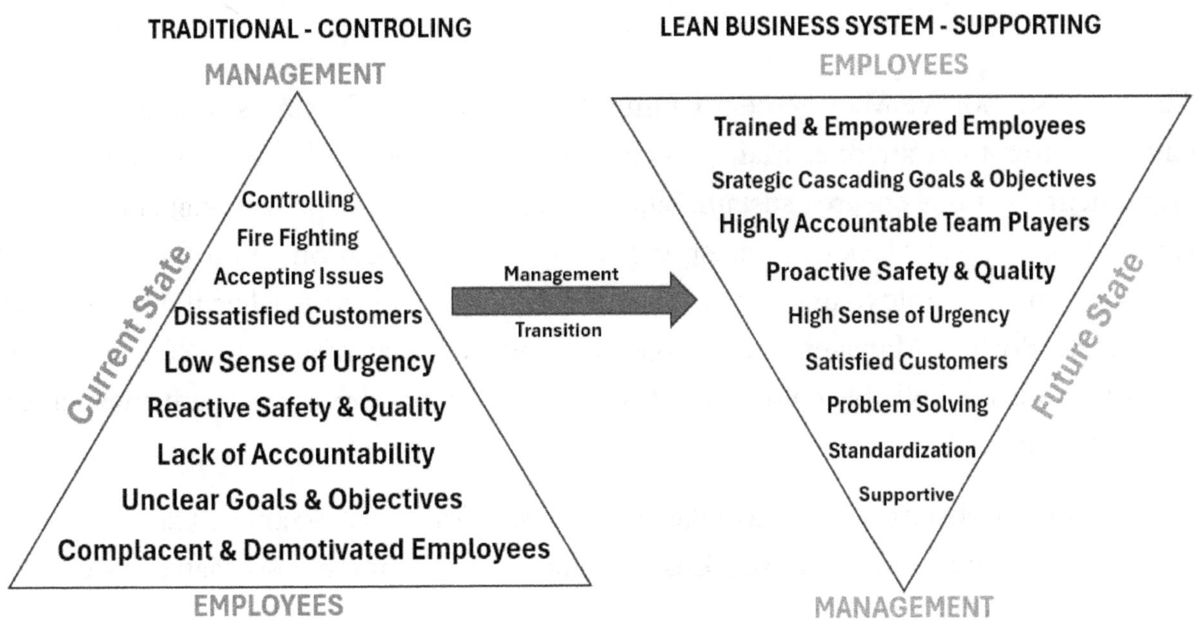

This hierarchy change does not happen from one day to the next. The velocity of transitioning the organizational hierarchy will be proportionate to the volume of consistent and committed management engagement. Also, management enthusiasm can be thought of as lubrication to increase velocity of the transition.

Another way to visualize this required management change from a Traditional Controlling Management Culture to a Lean Business System Supportive Management Culture is illustrated below.

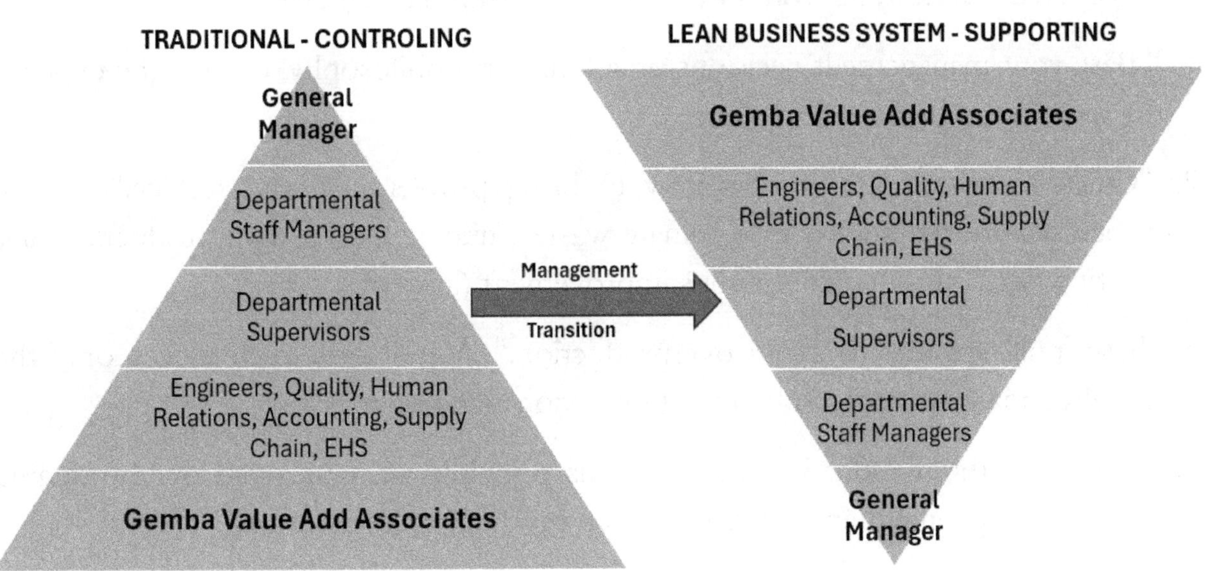

The Lean Supportive Management Culture knows the Lean Business System tools and culture better than anyone. Management engagement not only sponsors and drives implementation but ensures sustainability at every process step. If managers display a lack of knowledge or lack of interest, the rest of the organization will follow their lead. Managers must be able to understand the methodology, and to visualize the future state. Consistent Positive Management Engagement and Reinforcement is the "Lightening In a Bottle". It is the invisible cultural electricity in the air that drives associate engagement and satisfaction.

One simple jumpstart hack is to take the organization's management team to a peer group organization that is already Lean Business System mature so managers can see and feel what the future state looks like.

Lean Manufacturing Methodology

As previously stated, the Lean Business System is not just Lean Manufacturing Methodology, but it is essential for managers to understand the Methodology. Lean Methodology is deeply woven into the fabric of the Gemba and Kaizen cultural building blocks. Also, understanding, and teaching associates the Toyota Way 14 Principles will give an organization a jump start on the road to Lean Business System understanding since all 14 principals are embedded in the Lean Business System's five building blocks to be covered. The Toyota Way 14 Principles are summarized below:

1. "Base your management decisions on a long-term philosophy, even at the expense of short-term financial goals."

2. "Create a continuous process flow to bring problems to the surface." Work processes are redesigned to eliminate waste (muda), such as overproduction and waiting times, through continuous improvement (kaizen).

3. "Use 'pull' systems to avoid overproduction." A pull system produces only the required material after a subsequent operation signals a need.

4. "Level out the workload (heijunka). This principle aims to avoid overburdening people or equipment and creating uneven production levels (mura).

5. "Build a culture of stopping to resolve problems, to get quality right the first time." Quality takes precedence (Jidoka). Any employee can stop the process to signal a quality issue.
6. "Standardized tasks and processes are the foundation for continuous improvement and employee empowerment."
7. "Use visual control so no problems are hidden." This principle includes the 5S Program, steps that are used to make all workspaces efficient and productive, help people share workstations, reduce time looking for needed tools, and improve the work environment.
8. "Use only reliable, thoroughly tested technology that serves your people and processes."
9. "Grow leaders who thoroughly understand the work, live the philosophy, and teach it to others."
10. Develop exceptional people and teams who follow your company's philosophy."
11. "Respect your extended network of partners and suppliers by challenging them and helping them improve."
12. "Go and see for yourself to thoroughly understand the situation (Genchi Genbutsu)."
13. "Make decisions slowly by consensus, thoroughly considering all options; implement decisions rapidly (nemawashi)."
14. "Become a learning organization through relentless reflection (hansei) and continuous improvement (kaizen)."

***From Wikipedia, extract from the book "The Toyota Way" by Jeffrey Liker.*

It's no secret that there are thousands of articles and books expounding the subject of Lean Manufacturing. Also, there must be millions of certified and self-identified Lean Manufacturing Experts running around the globe. And yet, with all of this information and experts exhausting the subject, in many organizations the people (or positions) that need clarity of the information the most, in order to eliminate waste and optimize Safety, Quality, Delivery, and Cost performance appear to not understand the Methodology adequately. Positions such Finance Directors, Cost Accountants, Human

Relations, Supervisors and even the personnel actually turning the screws at Gemba do not have adequate knowledge of the tools and the culture required to consistently optimize results. How can this happen? Can't be for lack of information, plenty of that out there.

There is more than one reason as to why Lean Business System transformations fail. To prevent transformation failure, an organization must have a clear Lean Business System Strategy, and Execution planning to successfully implement and sustain the system. It should be a component of their Strategy Planning, Deployment, and Achievement processes.

Lean Manufacturing Methodology is the relentless reduction of waste in order to deliver Customer Value. Customer Value being defined as what the customer perceives as value and is willing to pay for. If the customer is not willing to pay for certain operations, the factory should not be doing those operations. There may be some exceptions to this rule, for example, additional internal testing for compliance certification, etc. But you get the general picture. Waste is additional cost that will go straight to the Profit & Loss Statement, and if not identified and eliminated, may cause the future loss of customers, revenue, and profit, due to an organization losing its competitive edge.

All Lean practitioners really need to educate themselves regarding their connection to the organization's Profit & Loss (Income Statement). A common criticism of Lean Practitioners is that they lack the Financial Acumen to be able to speak the language of "Financeze" when engaging with top echelon management. This lack of financial acumen must frustrate management and does nothing for the advancement of the organization's Lean Business System initiatives.

Impacted P&L accounts should be identified on the Lean Projects Kaizen Charters, which should be aligned with the Company's Site Improvement Planning, which should be aligned with the Annual Budgeting Process, which should be aligned with the organization's Strategy Deployment Planning, which should be aligned with the spirit of the organization's Vision & Values.

In order to relentlessly reduce waste and consistently improve performance stability, Lean Manufacturing Methodology employs a variety of tools (methodologies). Some of these Lean tools are shown below:

Andon
Heijunka
Waste Safari
TPM
5S
Standard Work
Continuous Flow
Bottleneck
One Piece Flow
JIT
VSM
Poka Yoke
SMED
TAKT TIME
KPI´s
OEE
Hoshin Kanri
Kaizen
RCCM
Jidoka
Kanban
Gemba Walk
Visual Factory
VA/VE
PDCA

This illustration is a bit confusing, but that is intentional. To the untrained practitioner, this illustration may look daunting. Like Lean Manufacturing snippets thrown together from multiple internet postings. But if we align these Lean tools with a Lean Strategy Roadmap and with the Lean Business System cultures, the Lean Tools start to fall right into place along the roadmap. The illustration below displays this concept better organized and much clearer.

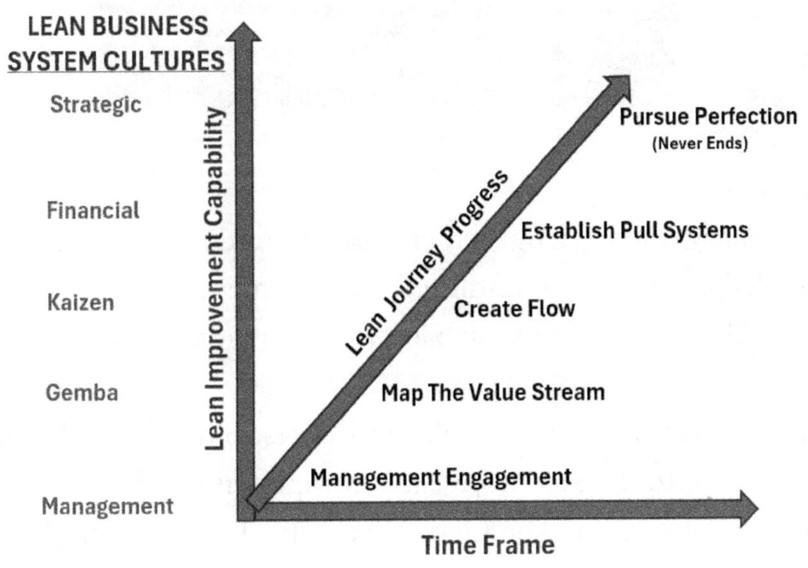

LEAN TOOLS

Hoshin Kanri, Strategy Deployment
Site Improvement Planning
Leader Standard Work
Root Cause/Countermeasure
Value Analysis/Value Engineering (VA/VE)
Total Productive Maintenance (TPM)
Single Minute Exchange of Dies (SMED)
Overall Equipment Efficiency (OEE)
Kanban Pull
Poka Yoke
Level Loading/Set up Wheel (Heijunka)
Continuous Flow
Value Stream Mapping
Rapid Response Escalation -QRQC
Gemba Methodology/Gemba Walk
Responsibility Board
Andon Escalation
Visual Factory
Daily Management
Standardized Work
5S/6S
8 Wastes
Leader Standard Work

The implementation of Lean Tools & Cultures is essential for the successful implementation of the Lean Business System, but they are not the whole of the Lean Business System. Lean Tools & Cultures are the heart of the "Gemba Culture" and "Kaizen Culture", and they are also key contributors to the Management, Financial, and Strategic building blocks cultures.

Let's look at the Lean Cultural building blocks in another way. The Toyota Production System House, an illustration that Lean Practitioners use as a Lean Manufacturing holy grail, can also be aligned with the Lean Business System Cultural Building Blocks.

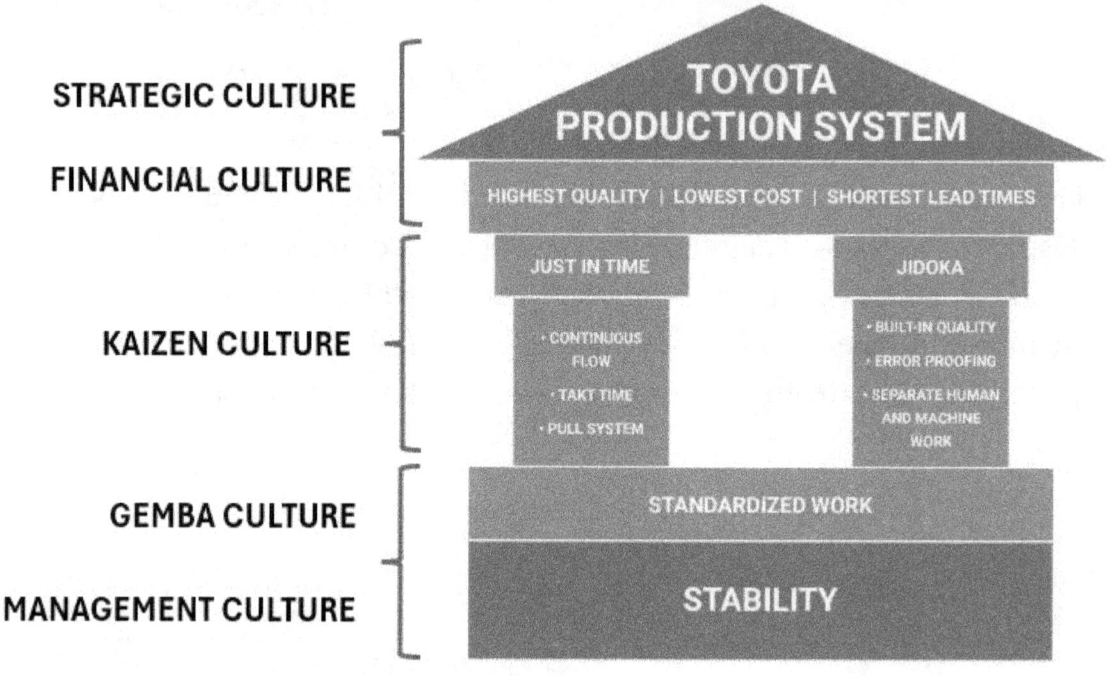

(1) **<u>Management Culture:</u>** Management Engagement is a critically necessary component. Without knowledgeable and committed Management Engagement, associates will not become fully engaged, and payback from initiatives will not be fully realized nor sustainable.

(2) **<u>Gemba Culture:</u>** Learning the Gemba Lean Tools, and developing the Cultural Empowerment to utilize those tools are necessary components of Stability. Standardized Work is a cornerstone tool in the Gemba Stability Tools arsenal, and may be present at Gemba in several different concepts.

(3) **Kaizen Culture:** The two Continuous Improvement Tools columns are components of Kaizen Culture and are critically important components for further waste/cost elimination beyond the Gemba Culture. Both Gemba and Kaizen Cultures waste elimination are key inputs into the organization's Site Improvement Planning.

(4) **Finance Culture:** Highest Quality, Lowest Cost, and Shortest Lead Times are all outputs from the Management, Gemba & Kaizen Cultures. and are analyzed, forecasted, and aligned to the requirements of the business stakeholders as part of the Finance Culture. The business stakeholders include Customers, Associates and Shareholders, and in some cases suppliers, and even the community in which the business is located. All of these stakeholders have different needs that must be addressed in the business financials.

(5) **Strategy Culture:** The house roof could be envisioned as the Strategy Culture. The overarching process to convert the organization's Mission, Vision and Values into Strategy Planning, Deployment, and Achievement actions through the other four Lean Business System building blocks. The business must have short term and longer term strategic initiatives, cascading deployment, and achievement planning assigned to accountable owners. Anything less, and the business deliverables can drift off course being eroded by surprise after surprise.

Lean Assessment

A good place to start the Management Tools & Culture journey would be an assessment of where the Management Culture of the business is now (current state). Depending on the size of the organization, this could be conducted by internal personnel or an external Lean Business System professional.

The assessment tool should refer to all of the topics included in the Lean Business System. Refer to the below assessment format as an example. The scoring tool is also just an example to demonstrate how the example format functions.

Lean Business System Assessment Example

(1) MANAGEMENT TOOLS & CULTURE	SCORING
Review of Mission, Vision, Values	2
Lean Business System Framework	3
Lean Leadership Training	3
Organization Hierarchy Accountability	4
Leadership Standard Work	3
Management Interviews	3
TOTAL AVERAGE SCORE	3

(2) GEMBA (At Gemba) TOOLS & CULTURE	SCORING
Accountability at Gemba (Associates, Leaders, Supervisors, Manager	3
Leading Metrics Stability	4
Associates Waste Reduction Knowledge	2
5S/6S Methodology	3
Visual Management	4
Process Standardization	3
Gemba Problem Solving Methodologies	3
Associate Lean & Skills Training (Training Matrix)	1
Gemba Quality Systems & Metrics	2
Associate Empowerment (Safety & Quality.	4
Associate Interviews	3
TOTAL AVERAGE SCORE	3

(3) KAIZEN (Gemba & Pursuit of Perfection Managen	SCORING
Continuous Improvement Culture Interviews	3
-Gemba Quality Costs	3
-Waste Elimination at Gemba	4
-Associates CI Ideas Program	2
-Profit & Loss Variations Knowledge	3
-Value Stream Mapping	3
-Gemba Process Flow	2
-Gemba Materials Flow (Push/Pull, Supermarkets, Points of Use)	2
-Overall Equipment Effectiveness (Metrics & Methodology)	2
-Single Minute Exchange of Dies	3
-Total Productive Maintenance (Preventative, Autonomous)	2
-Value Analysis, Value Engineering	2
Kaizen Events/Organization Kaizen Calendar	3
TOTAL AVERAGE SCORE	3

(4) FINANCE (Organization Education & Alignment)	
Organizational Profit & Loss Downstream Accountability	2
Budgeting Process	4
Key Financial Indicators Cascading Alignment & Compliance	3
Site Improvement Planning Process & Achievement	3
Site Improvement Planning & Budgeting Alignment	3
Finance Management Interviews	4
TOTAL AVERAGE SCORE	3

(5) STRATEGIC (Organizational Cascading Alignment)	
Mission, Vision, Values Strategy Alignment	3
Stakeholders 'Requirements	3
Top Level Key Performance Indicators Compliance	2
Strategy Planning, Deployment, & Achievement Process	2
Lean Business System Roadmap	2
TOTAL AVERAGE SCORE	2

(6) MATERIALS MANAGEMENT SYSTEMS/PROCESSES	
Sales & Operations Planning (S&OP)	3
Sales Forecasting	3
ERP & MRP Configuration (Set up Data) Leadtimes, Mfg Time, SS	3
A Plan For Every Part	2
Supplier Geographics	3
Supplier Managed Inventory, Consignment, Supplier Stocking	2
Supplier Assessments	4
Supplier Metrics -Supplier Quality	4
Supplier Metrics -Supplier On-time Delivery	4
TOTAL AVERAGE SCORE	3

SCORING LEGEND EXAMPLE:

1. Does Not Exist
2. Not Effective
3. Inadequately Effective
4. Effective-Meets Expectations
5. Effective-Exceeds Expectations

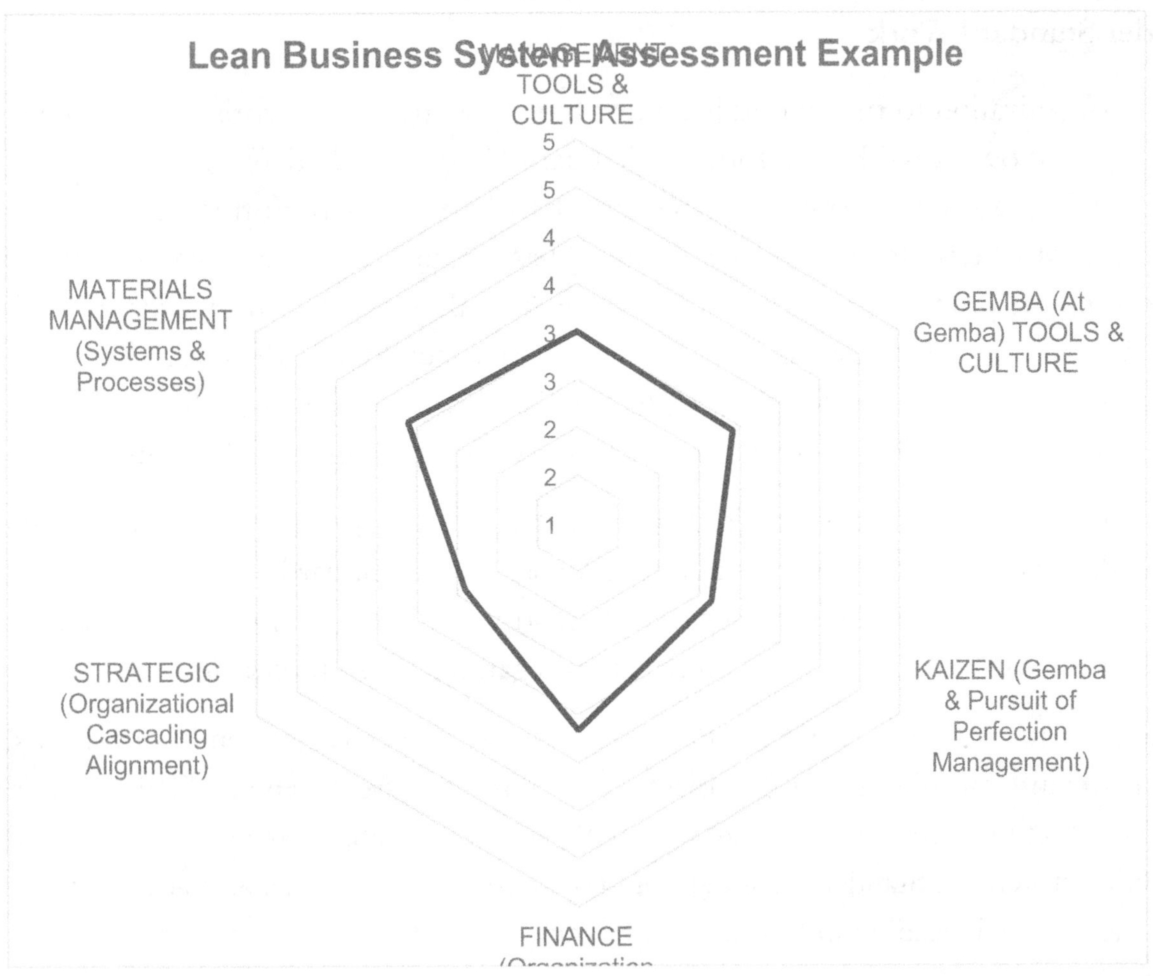

The above assessment example would also contain the detail of deficiencies found and recommended corrective actions.

There are many assessments tools available in the Lean Marketplace. Some are free, and some are for purchase from Lean Systems suppliers. Whether an organization uses an internally produced assessment or contracts a 3rd party assessment, the objective is to produce a clear understanding of current state and what additional actions are required to follow the Lean Business System Roadmap. After initial assessment, a project plan should be developed for actions timing to improve compliance to the Lean Business System Building Blocks future state.

Leader Standard Work

For an organization to run smoothly and with minimal negative surprises, everyone in the organization should have a form of Standard Work. Standard Work may come in different formats, and is essential to ensure that the work is performed consistently regardless of who performs it. Just as value add associates should have Standard Work to ensure that processes and products are consistently produced in accordance with customer specifications, so should Managers. Manager Standard Work should be designed to include tasks or activities that are critical to business performance and stakeholders' satisfaction. It is not intended to cover every minute of the working day.

One way to think of Leader Standard Work is that if a manager goes home at the end of the day without completing the assigned Management Standard Work Tasks, could this situation negatively affect business performance such as Daily Management Leading Indicators, or the flow of information regarding those Indicators.

Organizations that have Strategy Planning with top level lagging indicator KPI's, Downstream Cascading Leading Indicators Deployment, Achievement Planning, and Accountability Owners in place, are a step ahead in designing Management Standard Work. Management Standard work should concentrate on the tasks and activities that make accountable leading indicators compliance successful. These tasks and activities should be "checked off" by the user to ensure that all daily, weekly, and monthly due date tasks are completed and noted on the Standard Work format prior to finishing the workday. Ideally, Management Standard Work should accompany the user during the workday, either by paper or electronically, and be visible to the user's reporting superior either real time, or at end of shift.

Below is an example of a Management Standard Work format, but like all Visual Management Tools, Management Standard Work formats should be designed to meet the requirements of the business.

LEADER STANDARD WORK																											
January 2025																											
NAME:			POSITION:												UNIT:												
DAILY TASKS & ACTIVITIES			WEEK 1					WEEK 2					WEEK 3					WEEK 4					WEEK 5				
Start	Finish	Task or Activity	M	T	W	T	F	M	T	W	T	F	M	T	W	T	F	M	T	W	T	F	M	T	W	T	F
WEEKLY TASKS & ACTIVITIES			WEEK 1					WEEK 2					WEEK 3					WEEK 4					WEEK 5				
Start	Finish	Task or Activity	M	T	W	T	F	M	T	W	T	F	M	T	W	T	F	M	T	W	T	F	M	T	W	T	F
MONTHLY TASKS & ACTIVITIES			WEEK 1					WEEK 2					WEEK 3					WEEK 4					WEEK 5				
Start	Finish	Task or Activity	M	T	W	T	F	M	T	W	T	F	M	T	W	T	F	M	T	W	T	F	M	T	W	T	F

Associate Training & Engagement

Sending managers, supervisors, and associates to Gemba without a basic understanding of Gemba is starting them on the shop floor with a profound disadvantage. They will see a lot of value add and non-value activity occurring and they may not be able to segregate one from the other. Eventually they may figure it out, but eventually is not an optimal approach. All Associates need to understand the components that make up the Gemba & Kaizen Cultures. They need to be able to see wastes, and understand how to employ the Lean Tools associated with these Cultures. It is disappointing to visit a company that has spent thousands of dollars on Visual Management boards and monitors, but has no sustainable culture that understands the real purpose of those visual management tools.

Organizations that do not understand the Lean Tools and the associated Gemba and Kaizen cultural application are just going through the motions, checking the box, but never really realizing continuous sustainable improvements. This is exactly what gives Lean Business System Methodology an unfavorable perception to some higher echelon managers.

It is not practical to think that all of this knowledge can be learned and experienced in a day, but with consistent teaching, hands on experience, and relentless management engagement, most all associates can become highly engaged-high performance contributors to the Gemba & Kaizen Cultures.

Below is an illustration of a Continuous Lean Business System Tools & Cultures teaching curriculum example combining formal classroom & Gemba hands-on training. An associate could go around the training circle many times, having the opportunity of learning more advanced Lean & Six Sigma Tools as well as participating in and leading additional Kaizen events. These employees completing the circle become Lean highly engaged-high performance associates. They also have an opportunity to advance their careers through the Leader, Supervisor and Manager organizational hierarchy. The below example should provoke thoughts on how to design a sustainable training program that will benefit all stakeholders in the reader's organization.

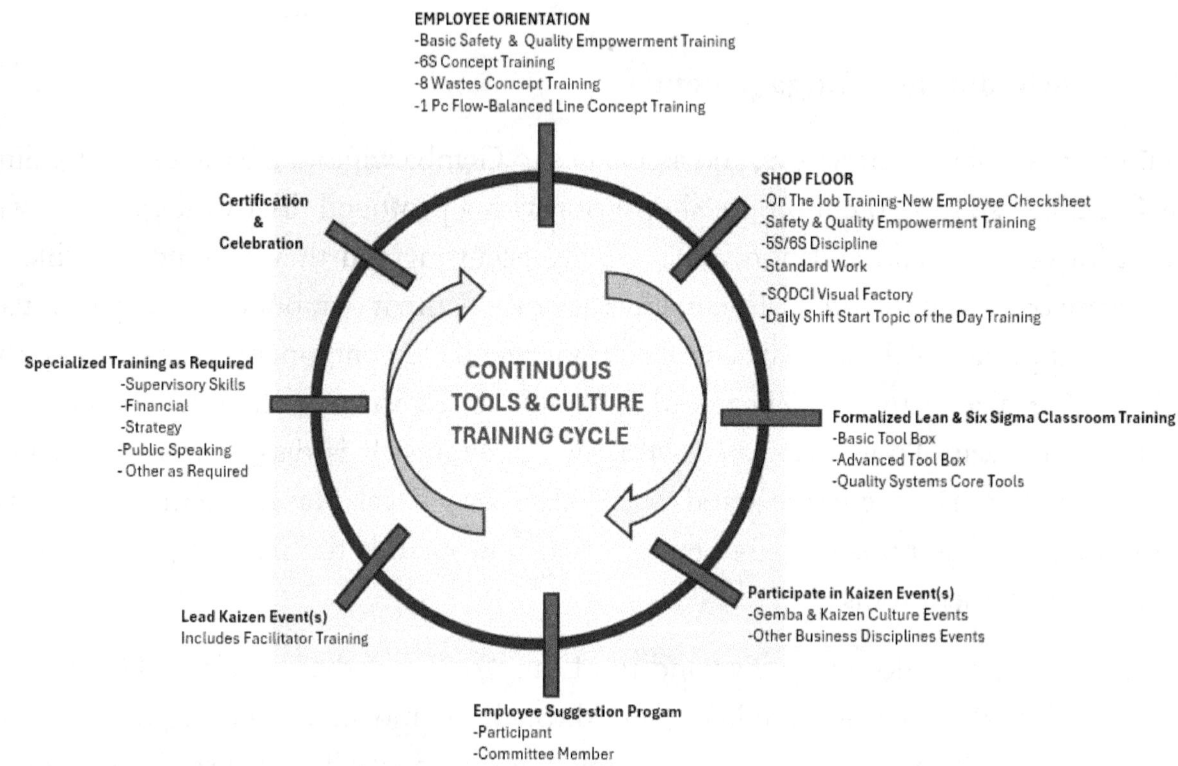

Safety, Quality, Delivery, Cost - A Management Compass.

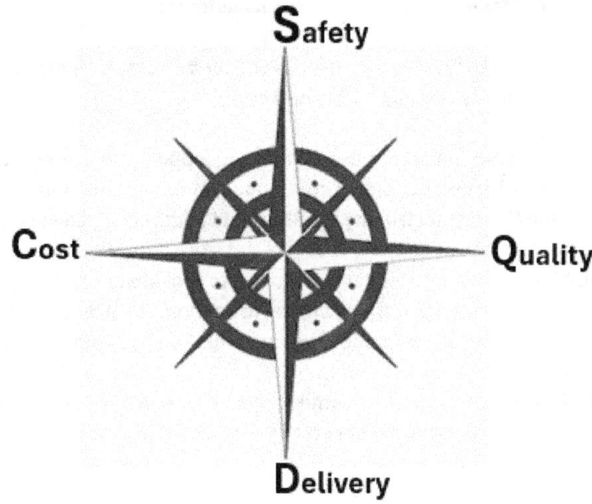

Lean Business System Managers should have a "Priority Compass" that is always their guide during short or long term planning, and in their day-to-day decisions that affect Safety, Quality, Delivery, & Cost. Strategy Initiatives and repetitive standardized work should have already considered these priorities, but it is the non-standardized work and unanticipated day-to-day decisions where the priority compass is useful. While Safety-Quality-Delivery-Cost may seem most applicable to Gemba Culture, it applies to every phase of the Lean Business System and to every business discipline in an organization.

For the unanticipated events that require unanticipated decisions, all personnel should use the Safety-Quality-Delivery-Cost compass as their guide. Some organizations may negotiate the priorities of Delivery and Cost given particular stakeholder situations, but Safety and Quality should NEVER be negotiated and should always be considered as 0 tolerance priorities.

EXAMPLE OF THE MANAGEMENT PRIORTY COMPASS

(1) SAFETY: Management committment that associate safety is <u>always</u> the number 1 priority.

(2) QUALITY: Management committment to always provide customer specified quality products 1st time. This includes external & internal customers.

(3) DELIVERY: Management committment to deliver customer´s products & services on time, without sacrificing Safety or Quality.

(4) COST: Management committment to lead, support and be engaged in the organization´s Lean Business Systems continuous improvement initiatives to produce products with the (1) Highest Quality (2) Shortest Leadtime (3) Lowest Cost

*WORKING CAPITAL: Management committment to provide the appropriate resources and systems to manage working capital in accordance with stakeholder expectations. (for the purpose of waste reduction, the primary focus would be inventory)

*ASSOCIATE MORALE: Management committment to provide a workplace environment that provides associate respect, engagement, and empowerment.

All of the compass priorities, including Working Capital and Associate Morale, should be measurable, and should be included in the organization's Strategy Deployment initiatives and cascading metrics.

Driving Associate Engagement and Satisfaction

It is Management's task to start the fire of the Engagement & Empowerment culture and keep that flame burning so that the destructive winds of complacency can never extinguish them. It is worth repeating:

"What is not important to Management,
will not be important to the rest of the organization"

But how does associate engagement happen? Management cannot demand it. They can request it, but without some substance of what and why they are asking for, the petitioned engagement soon fades away.

Although the lines separating associate engagement and associate satisfaction may at times seem blurred, they are distinctly different. Engaged Associates should develop a feeling or sense of belonging to an organization through an emotional connection that produces a degree of personal commitment. On the other hand, a satisfied employee may show up for work every day and think that the company is a nice place to work, but may have no emotional connection or feeling of belonging. In fact, as illogical as it may sound, sometimes satisfied employees can be the worst employees. Especially if management is not consistently engaged with them. These are the employees that may like the benefits, and may work their required hours, but go home and tell the family and friends how unengaged management is. These are also the employees that may see the waste issues first-hand, and if they somehow become engaged, they can be a storehouse of improvement suggestions.

Some companies get caught in the trap of chasing Employee Satisfaction when they really should be developing and following a roadmap of Employee Engagement. According to some research (Kenexa & Towers Perrin) companies with engaged employees have higher levels of profit.

There are many initiatives that can be implemented to jumpstart engagement and satisfaction. It is important to understand which are effective regarding Lean Business System associate engagement, and which are focusing more on associate satisfaction, while also understanding that some initiatives may accomplish both.

Below are some examples of initiatives focused on associate engagement and/or associate satisfaction. As with any associate initiatives, they should be tailored to meet the specific needs of the organization's Lean Business System journey. This is also a great example of why Human Relations resources should also be closely involved as Lean Business System experts.

Associate Engagement & Empowerment Initiatives

- Management Living The Company Values
- Safety Empowerment Program
- Quality Empowerment Program
- A Clean and Well Organized Working Environment
- Lean Business System Training
- Communication of Expectations & Results

- An Effective Gemba Methodology
- Employee Lean Improvement Ideas
- Kaizen Events Involvement
- Visual Management Tier Meetings
- Team Building Workshops
- Visiting Other Lean Organizations
- Performance Recognition & Reward
- Quarterly Performance Reviews
- Professional Growth Opportunities

Associate Satisfaction Initiatives

- Positive Employee Orientation
- Work/Life Balance environment
- A Respectful Working Environment
- Recognitions of Birthdays and Anniversaries
- Town Hall Type Communications
- Proactive Wellness Programs
- Employee Peer Recognition Programs
- Community Involvement Programs
- Family Day Recognition Programs

The organization's management team should develop an Engagement & Empowerment plan & implementation timeline. A Swimland top level planning tool can help to organize implementation timing. This tool will also be included in the Lean Business System Roadmap discussed in the Summary section.

Lean Business System IMPLEMENTATION CULTURAL SWIM LANES (example)

TOOLS & CULTURES	JANUARY	FEBRUARY	MARCH	APRIL	MAY	JUNE
MANAGEMENT		Town Hall	Town Hall	Town Hall	Town Hall	Town Hall
	Mgmt LBS Training			Mgmt LBS Training		
	LBS Site Visit			LBS Site Visit		
	Daily Gembas	Daily Gembas	Daily Gembas	Daily Gembas	Daily Gembas	Daily Gembas
GEMBA	2nd Level Training	Associate Gemba Training				
	Safety Empowerment	Quality Empowerment		Safety Empowerment	Quality Empowerment	
	Develop 6S Program	Implement 1S & 2S	Implement 3S & 4S	Implement 5S & 6S		
		6S Recognition	6S Recognition	6S Recognition	6S Recognition	6S Recognition
KAIZEN						
		Develop Kaizen Training	Associate KaizenTraining	Associate KaizenTraining	Associate KaizenTraining	Associate KaizenTraining
		Develop Site Imp Plan	Lean Suggestion Program	Lean Suggestion Program	Lean Suggestion Program	Lean Suggestion Program
		Weekly Kaizens	Weekly Kaizens	Weekly Kaizens	Weekly Kaizens	Weekly Kaizens
FINANCIAL	Mgmt Finance Training					
		Conduct P&L Drill Down	Conduct P&L Drill Down	Conduct P&L Drill Down	Conduct P&L Drill Down	Conduct P&L Drill Down
STRATEGY	Management	Management	Management	Management	Management	Management
	Review	Review	Review	Review	Review	Review

From the swim lane planning tool, the organization should move forward with more detailed implementation planning such as Gantt chart planning. A weekly scheduled Management Review of progress should be conducted to review implementation status and countermeasures (if required).

Failure is NOT an Option

It is important for Managers to understand that the reality of Lean Business System Transformation failure is real. According to a 2024 LinkedIn article by Value Driven Solutions, "*a study of manufacturers concluded that only 24% of Lean initiatives have accomplished significant results*". There are several failure pitfalls that managers should be aware of, but according to the study, the number one reason was lack of Senior Leadership Support.

Management Leaders must learn and understand the five Lean Business System Building Blocks Tools & Cultures, and chart an implementation plan and timeline. Once management is all in, there should be no going back. There is a teaching example regarding the way to conquer an island: *"Burn the boats upon arrival so that there is no way back"*. No plan B. There may be setbacks to deal with and adjustments along the way, but implementation of the Lean Business Systems plan should have no plan B. That should be the Lean Business System management mantra and attitude.

"Burn the Boats - Enjoy the Journey"

UNIT 2 - GEMBA TOOLS & CULTURE

Gemba Culture - Business Performance Stabilization

Gemba Methodology

What is Gemba? In simple terms, it is where the work is being performed. The real place. It is where the real Value Add, or in many cases where the real Non-Value Add (waste) is occurring. This unit's discussion is primarily focused on manufacturing, but Gemba can be anywhere. For example, in a hospital operating room. The surgeon and the immediate operating assistants are the value add operators. Similar Safety, Quality, Delivery, and Cost operating theater concepts and attributes of the Lean Business System still apply.

Gemba Methodology is a contributor to Gemba culture and is not to be confused with Gemba Walking, although Gemba Walking is also a contributor to Gemba Methodology. Gemba Methodology runs much broader and deeper than just Gemba Walking. Gemba Methodology is the structural steel that holds together the House of Gemba. The closer one is to Gemba (where the value add work is being performed), the more frequent one should be present at Gemba and be a caretaker of the value add processes that take place there. An advocate and protector of Gemba Safety, Quality, Delivery and Cost.

The illustration below shows a manufacturing Gemba Methodology example. The shown Gemba Methodology positions would be tailored to the actual positions of a company's organization chart.

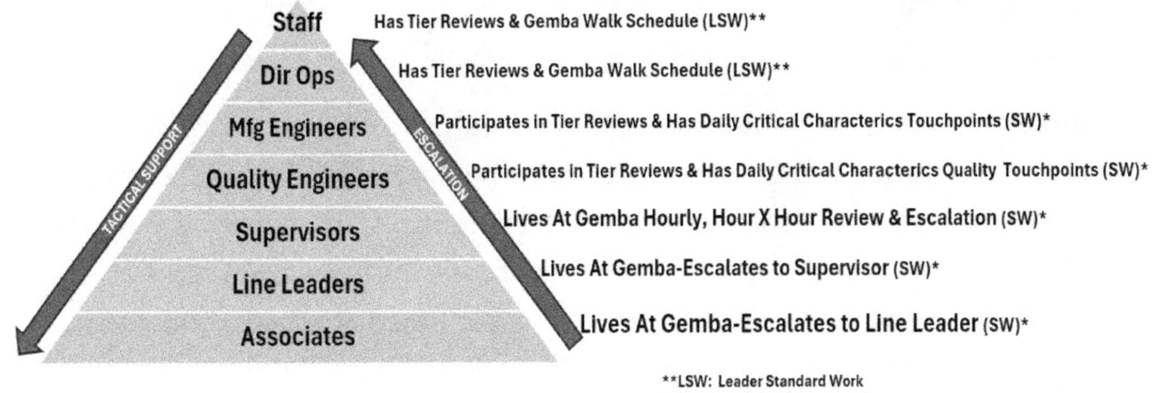

This example illustrates Gemba Methodology on a manufacturing floor and shows that Gemba is the responsibility of many. All should have standard work as it pertains to their responsible processes that contribute to success at Gemba. Each of the Gemba Methodology participants have an opportunity to favorably influence the Value Add Work at Gemba by ensuring that processes and quality standards are strictly adhered to, and that the opportunities for improvement are captured. This methodology also unites an organization and promotes an environment of teamwork and positive morale. Associates can actually see for themselves that everyone is consistently involved in the achievement of common Value Add goals, derived from cascading Strategy Planning goals and Standard Work.

An organization will need to tailor their Gemba Methodology to their particular business, but the same rules apply to all organizations.

- The closer one is to Gemba, the more time and caretaking spent at Gemba.
- The Safety, Quality, Delivery, & Cost goals are always clear and visible.
- Everyone has Standard Work pertaining to their Value Add responsibility at Gemba.
- Every time one is at Gemba, it should be considered as an opportunity to positively interface with team members and look for improvement opportunities. An attitude of *"What can we improve today"?*

Gemba Methodology Touch Points

Gemba Touch Points may be thought of as an additional layer of flexible auditing standard work. For organizations that are building their Safety, Quality, Delivery, &

Cost cultures, Touch Points may be used as a 'safety net' to prevent escapes until permanent safequards are in place and verified sustainable.

For example, Supervisors, Manufacturing Engineers, and Quality Engineers all have their day-to-day assigned job description tasks to perform. But 'Touch Points' can be applied to assure that items such as critical characteristics, or recent outputs from a Quality Circles session, or a recent engineering process change, are well implemented and being adhered to. A Quality Engineer responsible for an area with 30 assembly cells (or any operations) might have a Gemba Methodology Touch Point to visit two cells every day for a critical quality characteristic verification, or to verify effectiveness of a recently changed Quality Systems process.

Touch Points can be applied to any Gemba participant, including administrative back office participants. Gemba Touch Points should be a form of flexible Standard Work scheduling, similar to the Management Gemba Walk Schedule. Flexible, meaning it can change as the need for a Touch Point verification changes. Also, Touch Point schedules, like Gemba Walk schedules should be visibly posted and completion checked off on a daily basis.

Management Gemba Walking

There are many positive aspects regarding the Management Gemba Walk, but contrary to the published beliefs of many practitioners, it is not intended to cure world hunger on the manufacturing floor. There are two principal goals of the Management Gemba Walk:

- Engage with employees, understand their Safety, Quality, Delivery, and Cost (Productivity) concerns, and provide the appropriate support for those concerns.
- Gain an understanding if the organization's Gemba Methodology is effective. It is Gemba Methodology that should be designed to cure world hunger on the manufacturing floor, not the management Gemba Walk. Management cannot be everywhere at once, but Gemba Methodology provides the everywhere at once advantage. If Safety, Quality, Delivery, & Cost deficiencies are evident during the Management Gemba Walk, that is a symptom of a lack of Gemba Methodology effectiveness in a particular area of Gemba responsibility, and should be immediately addressed.

There are some guidelines to follow during the Management Gemba Walk:

- Employees should be treated with respect and professional empathy. If a Gemba issue is discovered during the walk, it is usually not their fault, but a standards deficiency or a Gemba Methodology deficiency.
- A checklist should accompany management on the walk. Checklists can be prepared to cover specific 5S/6S, Safety, Quality, Delivery, & Cost topics related to the areas to be walked. The inclusion of a checklist is not designed to be a reading exercise, but a reminder to cover all of the intended topics. The Gemba checklist should be fluid. For example, if the organization is just embarking on 5S and this week´s exercise is 1S, then 1S would be a checklist topic, not the whole 5S/6S methodology review.
- Area Gemba Methodology responsible personnel must be present on the walk.
- Allow associates, line leaders, and supervisors to guide the management team through the walk in their area. An associate reviewing a Safety-Quality-Delivery-Cost Visual Management Board with the management team is great for positive associate engagement.
- Both positive and negative findings should be reviewed. Positive findings may be an area to replicate for overall Gemba improvement, and negative findings to apply adequate root cause and countermeasures.
- The Gemba walk is also an opportunity for "extra points" inquiries such as "can you tell me the Safety Policy", or "what do you do in the case of a safety or quality issue?" Extra points inquiries are a positive method to build employee engagement, and to assess the organization's orientation and training processes.

Stability at Gemba

As previously mentioned, Gemba Culture needs to be functioning to some degree before Kaizen culture can begin to really reap and sustain the desired benefits. Gemba Culture brings stability to the value add areas and to the business. Every practitioner has probably heard, or has learned the hard way that it can be very difficult to improve in an unstable environment. Working to make Kaizen improvements in an unstable environment can seem futile at times because waste (Profit & Loss leakage) can overshadow improvements. At the end of the month the Profit & Loss operating profit shows no improvement even though the organization executed Kaizen Events. How can that be? This is an unpleasant question that organizational management will be required to answer.

Untrained associates and the lack of Gemba tools and Gemba Culture cannot sustain Kaizen improvements and will continue to create additional waste as illustrated below.

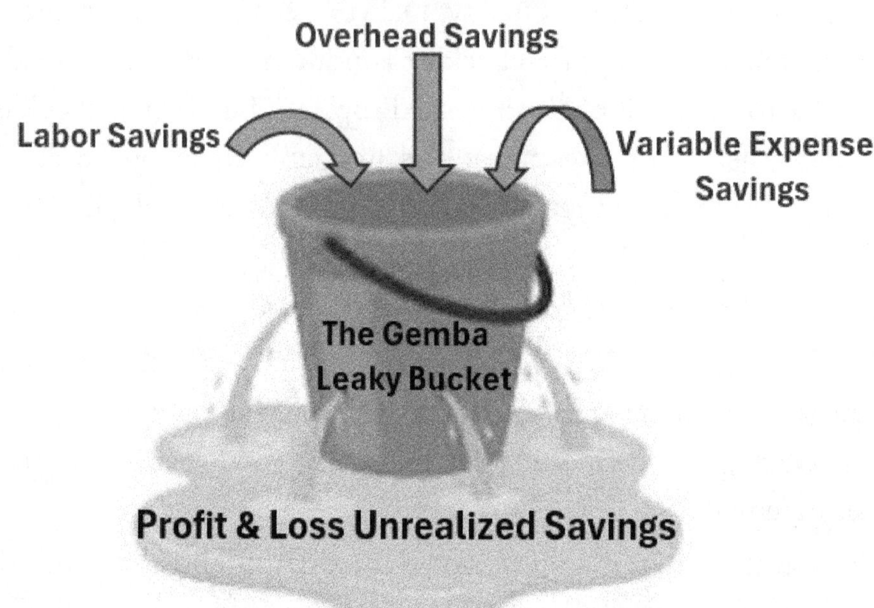

Unstable Gemba performance regarding Safety, Quality, Delivery, and Cost has real effects on the organization's Profit & Loss (Income Statement), and to its Stakeholders. Safety directly affects associates´ health & welfare, and operating costs. Quality and Delivery directly affects customers confidence and organizational operating cost. Poor productivity and other Gemba waste affects shareholders returns. Furthermore, all of these factors can affect the ability to maintain customers, affecting revenue.

The inability to stabilize Gemba can be a continual "cause & effect" cycle of poor Gemba indicators performance, stakeholder's dissatisfaction, and unfavorable profit & loss results. A Profit & Loss responsible manager´s perfect storm nightmare.

Every activity, or lack of, at Gemba will show up on the organization's Profit & Loss Statement, either favorably or unfavorably, and will directly affect the organization's stakeholders. Gemba production time resolution is not in minutes or hours, but in seconds or fractions of a second. And every second has a forecasted holding place on one of the many Profit & Loss financial accounts.

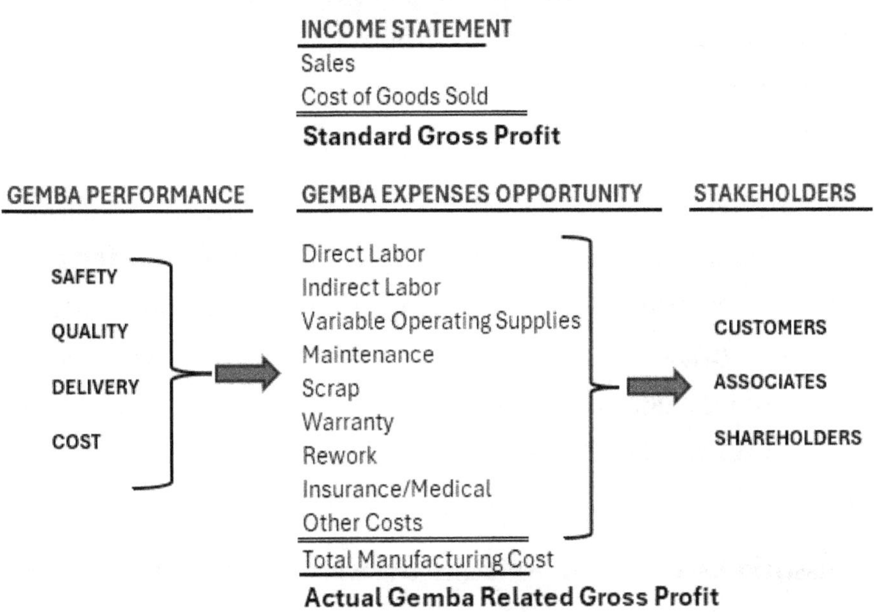

There is a well-known published story regarding Taiichi Ohno, one of the founding fathers of the Toyota Production System. When he was assigned a new engineer to train and mentor, he would go to Gemba and draw a circle on the floor near a production area and have the new engineer stand in the circle for maybe hours. Then Ohno would ask the engineer what he observed during his time in the circle. If Ohno was satisfied with the engineer's observations and suggestions, the engineer could leave the circle, if not, the engineer would have to repeat the process.

This is a very important point to consider regarding Gemba. When someone (especially an untrained someone) walks onto the Gemba production floor, they may see what looks like only value add activity occurring. But depending on the Lean maturity of the organization, there could also be a great amount of non-value add (waste) occurring at the same time. To an untrained eye, this waste may appear to be Value Add. Everyone may be busy, and the waste is so well woven into the fabric of the process that the waste is not perceived at all to the untrained eye. This is what is referred to as the "Hidden Factory". The hidden factory appears different to everyone, depending on their experience and training. In other words, their ability to see waste.

The ability to see waste is crucial to the foundation of the Lean Business System. The Gemba Culture and Kaizen Culture transformations depends on eliminating waste and making improvements across all organization business disciplines. It will be very difficult to eliminate waste and make sustainable improvements if associates cannot see and identify waste. The ability to see waste should improve for associates that are closer to Gemba, but this is not always the case.

In the movie "Terminator", there is a scene in which the audience has an opportunity to see what the terminator is visualizing through his Terminator Vision. In this scene gauges, dials and messages appear to identify what he is seeing. Managers should think along the same lines regarding how to develop the organization's Waste Terminators. Terminator Vision is similar to how associates should learn to see waste at Gemba. Of course, they won't see gauges and dials, but they will be able to see and classify waste. Better still, they will understand the Gemba Culture and Kaizen Culture Tools used to reduce the waste.

But so many associates continue to walk by waste due to inadequate training, or inadequate engagement, or both. Gemba waste is not just important to shop floor associates, the Lean Business System Methodology requires that all associates be able to see process waste, at least in their respective departments. A successful Lean Business System transformation will permeate all departments and touch all personnel. Just imagine a manufacturing organization in which Supervisors and Managers cannot see wastes.

The Value Add of Gemba Culture is what SHOULD be consistently happening every second, every minute, every hour, of every day. This Value Add activity should be occurring in such an organized, standardized, and disciplined manner that Gemba incrementally becomes a stable environment with a minimum amount of waste. As this happens, Kaizen savings have visibility on the Profit & Loss without being overshadowed by the excessive costs of Gemba wastes.

It is worth repeating that 'you can't improve in an unstable environment'. While that statement has different degrees of accuracy depending where an organization is at in their Lean Business System Journey, if they do realize improvements, these improvements will most likely be short term and not sustainable. There are just too many unplanned issues to juggle in an unstable environment.

Just as the Toyota Production System House shows Stability as the foundation of the Toyota Production System, so is the case with the "House of Gemba Management" from Masaaki Imai in his book "Gemba Kaizen" highlighting Visual Management, Waste (Muda) Reduction & Standardization as foundations the Gemba House.

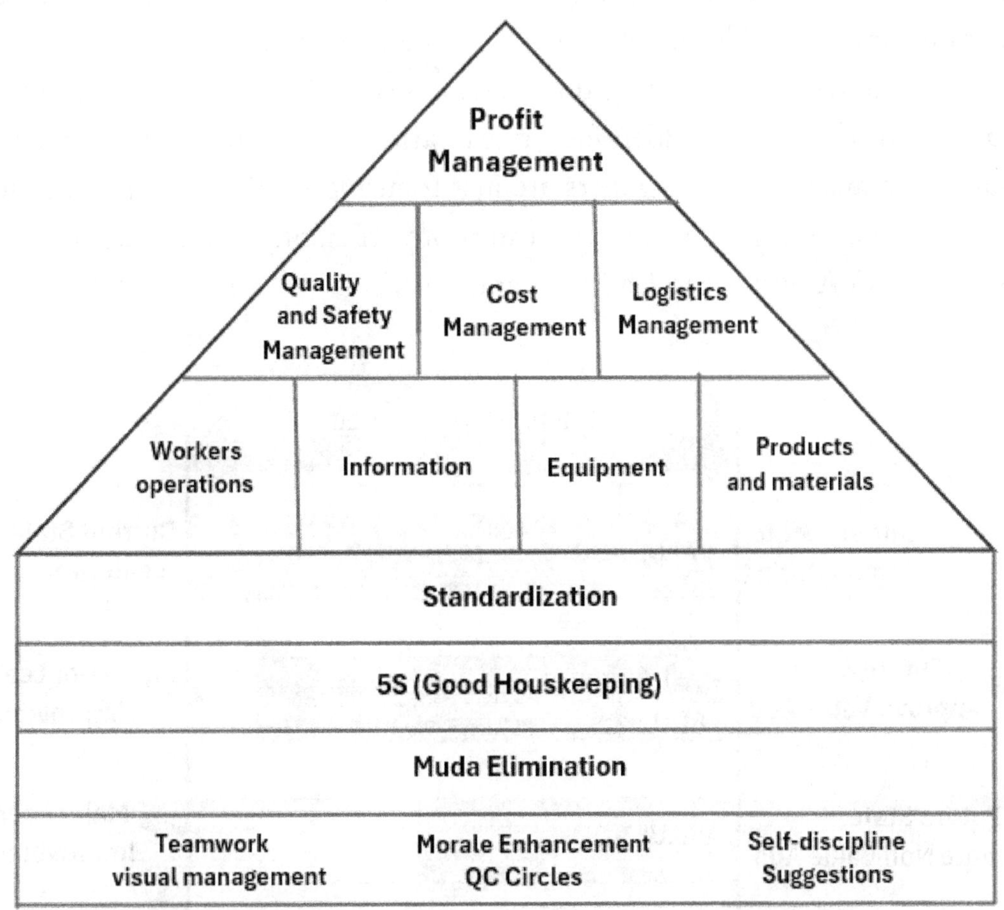

The House of Gemba Management

While a Lean Business System Assessment is a valuable tool to gauge a company's progress on their Lean Business System journey, it is Gemba that tells the tale. When one walks out onto a manufacturing plant production floor, almost immediately, one can see, hear, and almost feel the environment. The work areas are clean, well delineated, and well organized and there is no unnecessary WIP inventory laying around. Associates are engaged, productive, and production flow is visible. The Safety, Quality, Delivery, and Cost Visual Management tools are being used and display the current state of the business, highlighting additional activities to be completed in the never ending journey of pursuing perfection.

Eliminating Waste At Gemba

Recognizing and eliminating waste is critically important. Eliminating waste is a win/win for all stakeholders. Highest Quality, Shortest Lead Time, and Lowest Cost are all beneficiaries. In addition, eliminating waste really makes associate's work easier and more productive by eliminating unnecessary non-value added work. Shown below is an illustration of how the hidden factory can affect an organization. Especially if the organization's managers and engineers are just focusing on the known value add (VA) operations, such as trying to make them run more efficiently and faster, and not seeing the real waste (NVA) impact to lead time and cost.

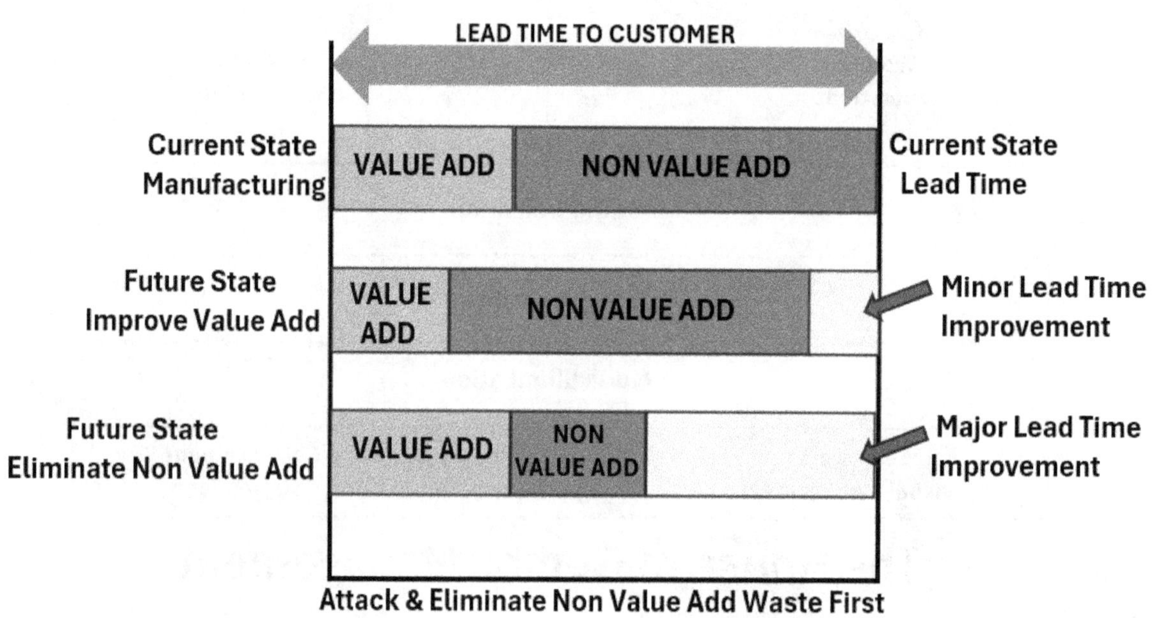

The elimination of non-value wastes in processes at Gemba has major effects on Safety, Quality, Delivery, Cost. Also, when associates see that the organization is engaged in the effort to improve processes and make their job easier, associate engagement and associate satisfaction improves.

Eight Types of Gemba Wastes - Plus a 9th.

There are two top classifications of waste in an organization. Unacceptable, and what a business may deem as necessary and acceptable to ensure, for example, business legal compliance or product integrity. This may be in the form of additional documentation of destructive testing or additional processes to ensure compliance. Of course, all waste should be scrutinized, even what has been deemed necessary, as it may reveal a gap or weak point in a design or process. This is especially valid for older products and processes. Changing technologies in product design, processing, materials, and quality detection may require a fresh new look at what was previously deemed as necessary & acceptable waste.

There are eight classical wastes published in almost every Lean Manufacturing manual or article. Lean practitioners have these eight wastes etched in their minds, and that is great. Unfortunately, that is not always true of everyone else working at Gemba, or responsible for the Safety, Quality, Delivery, Cost results at Gemba. Below is an overview of these eight classical waste. The bad news is that these eight wastes do exist. The good news is that the Lean Business System toolbox has a tool to reduce or eliminate most all business wastes.

- **Waiting:** Personnel and machines should never be waiting on anything. Waiting is one of the easiest wastes to spot. Anyone walking the shop floor and observes personnel or machines in the idle state should ask the question why. This also includes personnel waiting on machines to cycle. The why may be a perfectly acceptable temporary answer, or may be waste that should be immediately escalated, counter measured, and long term corrective action applied.

- **Defects:** Defects should never be acceptable. Like waiting, it is value immediately leaked from the Gemba stability bucket. Organizations typically accept some financial level of defects. But just because defects costs may be in line with a financial budget or even factored into the Material Requirements Planning system, neither should be readily accepted as a normal way of doing business.

- **Overproduction:** Overproduction is a waste of valuable resources (labor, materials, overhead) and can unfavorably affect performance indicators. Overproduction uses capacity that should have been used for another priority, and the additional overproduction waste will certainly show up as cost of excess inventory, warehouse space, and labor cost in the organization's Profit & Loss.

- **Inventory:** Inventory should be thought of as being naturally evil. Although a certain level of inventory is needed somewhere at some time, that amount of inventory should be managed to an absolute minimum. In an ideal world, the supplier owns any necessary inventory, delivers it to the point of use only as needed, finished products are immediately produced and shipped. In an ideal scenario, customer and supplier payment terms are negotiated so that the organization receives payment prior to having to pay the supplier, resulting in favorable cash flow. The Supply Chain "plan for every part", should be designed as close to utopia as possible in order to meet financial stakeholder's objectives.

- **Motion:** The less the better. Motion is time and time is cost. Production lines and work centers should be ergonomically designed and balanced to require a minimum of motion. The customer should not be expected to pay for excess motion. Associates should not be expected to suffer the ergonomic maladies caused by poor workstation design.

- **Excess Processing:** Overprocessing could be defined as providing more product attributes than the customer requires or is willing to pay for. Thus, making the product potentially uncompetitive. There are tools in the lean toolbox to attack this issue, such as: Design for Lean and Value Analysis/Value Engineering (VA/VE). Overprocessing may become more of a savings opportunity as design, materials, and manufacturing technologies change.

- **Transportation:** Anytime anything is transported anywhere, there is a cost involved. From a raw material supplier to a sub-supplier or direct to the producing factory. From the receiving dock to the warehouse. From the warehouse to the production floor. No transportation is free and should always be evaluated as an improvement opportunity.

- **Non-Utilized Talent:** This can be a double-sided waste. (1) Not using trained talent in the right place, which due to labor availability may sometimes be justified. (2) Using untrained talent in the wrong place, which can cause a multitude of Safety, Quality, Delivery, & Cost issues. The better educated and trained an organization is, the more agile the organization will be to prevent this type of waste.

- The Ninth Waste: The eight wastes reviewed above are core wastes plaguing the hidden factory and are wastes that a manufacturing floor or other value add organizations must work to reduce and eliminate. But anything that could negatively affect the organization's Profit & Loss should be considered a waste and should certainly be considered on the organization's Site Improvement Plan (to be discussed in Kaizen & Financial Cultures). For example, the contractual relationships with Customers and Suppliers should be monitored closely for wastes that may arise from commodity index decreases, expired pricing agreements, procurement contracts, etc. Every administrative department should look inward and self-evaluate the possibility of having a "9th" waste reduction opportunity.

5S/6S Methodology

There are no beautification projects in Lean Manufacturing. "But what about 5S" one misguided non practitioner may inquire, showing their real lack of understanding of the true benefits of the 5S methodology. If implemented and sustained correctly, the results of the program will certainly show up in the organization's Profit & Loss in short order.

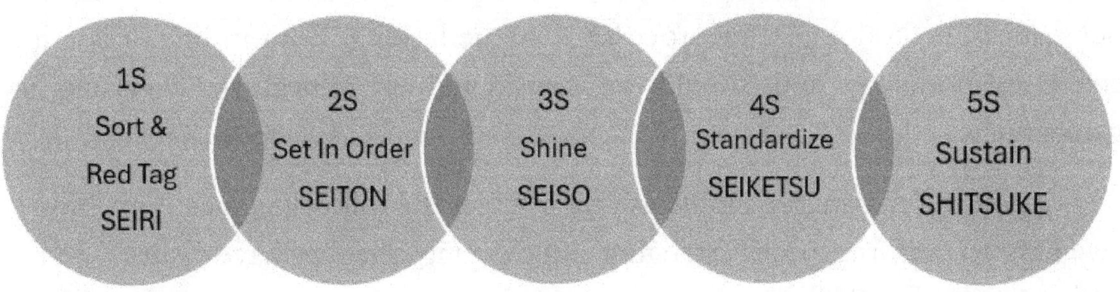

With the exception of someone living on an isolated island, a high percentage of the working population has probably heard the term 5S. But that percentage declines when asked to name the 5S's, and declines even more when asked to describe each of the 5S's, and even more when asked to articulate the real value of the 5S's. Also, practitioners may call the 5S's by different names in different languages, but the methodology should remain the same. Some people may describe the 5S methodology as a cleaning program. This misnomer may originate from the fact that a properly maintained 5S area is definitely clean and organized. But 5S is certainly more than just a cleaning program.

But why is 5S so important that almost everyone has heard of it? Simply, it is considered by many as being the most important tool in the Lean toolbox. If implemented and sustained correctly, it's almost immediate contribution to Safety, Quality, Delivery, Cost and Employee Morale is felt, seen, and heard. The effects of the methodology ripples favorably through several Profit & Loss account lines. But it goes even deeper than these aforementioned favorable effects. The methodology is considered a baseline contributor to STABILITY and STANDARDIZATION, two foundations of the Toyota Production System House of Lean. Lean practitioners are taught (or should be) that if an organization cannot sustain 5S methodology, it will most likely be unable to sustain other important initiatives. But if an organization can understand the value of the methodology and sustain it, they are a milestone step ahead on their Lean Business System journey.

5S done correctly is the baseline for future organizational discipline, standardization, accountability, and empowerment in general. The condition of an organization's 5S program speak volumes regarding management's engagement and conviction to Gemba. When an auditor, any program auditor, walks the floor of a manufacturing, distribution, or office area and observes poor 5S practices, they are instantly alerted that other critical methodologies or processes may be lacking. Bottom line, it is critical to Gemba methodology and should be considered as critical by everyone in the organization.

Every organization manager should ask themselves the following question: "How often do we have to perform special arranging and cleaning when we have visitors"? The next question should be: "Why"?

A brief description of the 6S's is below. There are many books, articles, and visual examples available to aid an organization embarking on this initiative.

1S Sort: Take an inventory of EVERYTHING in the assigned work area. Items that are not required should be removed from the area. Separate trash from the items that may have value, or use in other areas. Unnecessary Items with value should go to a designated Red Tag area. Companies should have a process of Red Tag disposal, to include proper identification, tag identification, review for use in other areas, financial disposition, and appropriate disposal. The Red Tag area should only be used for correctly processed and tagged items, not used as a general uncontrolled storage or disposal area. The Red Tag area should have assigned responsibility ownership and be included in the Gemba Methodology and Management Gemba Walk processes.

2S Set In Order: The 2S is commonly referred to as 'A Place For Everything and Everything in its Place'. Items remaining from the 1S exercise should have a visually assigned place and when items are not in use, they should remain in their 'Place'. Ideally items should be placed as close to the 'point of use' as possible. Reference the waste of Motion. Excessive reaching is not ergonomically desirable or healthy for associates and also causes excessive motion waste. Consider using external shadow boards or drawers with internal shadow boards, delineated areas with paint/tape, etc. The intent is that required items are always available, or there is a visible empty space if unavailable.

3S Shine: This means exactly how it sounds. Clean the area until it shines. Scrub the floor, the walls, the equipment, repaint as needed, etc. But the team should go a step further. If there is a root cause for continual dirtiness, find the root cause and make it go away. For work cells/areas on the shop floor, sometimes the space between these cells may not get enough 3S attention because there is no assigned owner. The use of a small piece of delineation tape to indicate where one area's responsibility ends and another begins is a simple way to maintain the cleaning boundaries. It is important that all areas have a responsible owner, and there is sustainable standard work, such as a daily cleaning routine, and that cleaning utensils are always available. A cleaning utensil shadow board is a good method to visualize if there are deficiencies of cleaning utensils.

4S Standardize: Organizations ideally should already have standardization policies and processes. This could mean standardized colors, taping schemes, shadow boards, SQDCI boards, formats for control plans, work instructions, inspection sheets, etc. If an organization does not already have this type of standardization, immediately would be a good time to start. Depending on where a company is in their Lean Business System journey, consider using a pilot cell/area to establish a 5S master cell example. A 5S boot camp is also a good way to involve and educate associates how to initiate, standardize, and sustain the program.

5S Sustain: Safety aside, sustain is perhaps the most important S. The organization must have sustaining aids and measures in place. Sustain aids could be daily 5S/6S check sheets, daily cleaning routines, cleaning utensils shadow boards, or area weekly 5S inspections with scoring, recognition and rewards, or a picture of the ideal 5S condition.

5S/6S should also be included in the Gemba Methodology and Management Gemba Walk processes. There are many ideas and tools to aid the sustainability process.

Starting the 5S methodology and failing to maintain it will quickly erode associate confidence and engagement in the 5S/56S program, as well as other programs, and create a flavor of the month" attitude. On the other hand, a sustained Safe, Clean and Efficient working environment does wonders for everyone's engagement and morale.

6S Safety (Environmental, Health & Safety): The Sixth S should be added to a 5S methodology program as quickly as possible. But the Sixth S should not just be added on without substance. Safety measures, both proactive, and post corrective, should be measurable and treated in all areas as the most critical metric. It should be included in almost everything an organization does. Safety should be the first metric and first discussion in the daily toolbox meetings and in all tier level meetings. Production areas should have 6S start up formats to ensure checking of guards, safety devices, chemical labeling, etc. Associates should have no doubt that in the event of a perceived safety/environmental issue, they can STOP the area and immediately ESCALATE. They must be empowered to do so, and the organization must treat safety as a 0 tolerance mindset.

An organization should view everything through the Environmental, Health, and Safety perspective and weave Safety into the fabric of everything they do. An added idea to keep safety culture on everyone's mind is to create a slogan that everyone knows and uses. For example, every meeting (office or manufacturing floor) could be opened with a safety culture slogan. "SAFETY FIRST, SAFETY ALWAYS" or other similar safety centric slogan.

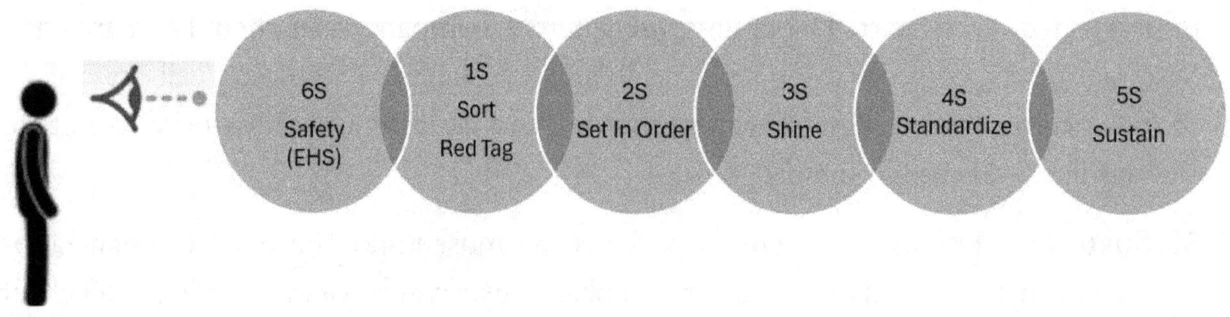

There are several methods to aid 5S/6S sustainability, such as:

- 5S/6S training for all employes. The methodology should be applicable to all organizational areas, including the production floor and all indirect and office areas. A 5S/6S methodology overview at Employee Orientation is an excellent way to prepare employees before entering the workplace.
- A 5S/6S benchmark photo for each area. When employees finish their areas´ initial 5S/6S transformation, a photo can be taken and posted in the area as a sustainability benchmark.
- A daily 5S/6S activity check sheet. This can include a quick check of each "S" and the cleaning routine. If multiple employees are in a production cell for example, the checklist and cleaning routine can be designated by employee 1, employee 2, and so on, so the employees can rotate doing different tasks of the checklist. Rotating 5S/6S tasks gives employees the opportunity to know all tasks well and to prevent burnout from doing the same tasks day after day.
- Weekly 5S/6S area inspections. These inspections can be self-audited or periodically audited by an employee from another area. This exercise becomes more feasible if all employees are trained and active in their own 5S/6S program. Also, a weekly or monthly recognition and reward goes a long way to keep employees interested and engaged in sustainability.
- Allowing time for the employees to complete their daily 5S/6S tasks. It is easy for managers and supervisors to become focused on production first and change the order of SQDC to CSQD. Appropriate management engagement at Gemba should prevent this from occurring.
- Making sure that employees have the tools and materials required for sustainability success. The visual cleaning tools shadow board is an easy way for employees and supervisors to monitor if all cleaning utensils are always available. Employees will become quickly disengaged if they want to be a model 5S/6S example but cannot get adequate support. On individual production or area tier boards a good idea is to have some type of "Rapid Response" list so cell employees can list items that the cell requires to be Safety, Quality, Delivery, & Cost successful. This "Rapid Response" list should have a task, assigned responsible, and an anticipated date to fulfill. This is an item that should be reviewed daily during Gemba Methodology and Management Gemba Walks to ensure that fulfilment dates are completed or adjusted if necessary.

- An important 5S/6S engagement item is the Gemba Methodology itself. Anytime a manager, supervisor, engineer, etc is in the Gemba area, they should be 5S/6S trained and able to help employees be successful by positively engaging with them.

6S methodology, or lack of, will favorably or unfavorably impact and organization. It will never be neutral.

Visual Management – Visual Factory

"That which is measured improves.
That which is measured and reported improves exponentially."

Karl Pearson

Two types of Visual Management.

- Visual Information: Provides information but does not require an escalation action by the observer. For example, a 5S poster, or tracking metric for information only, a building egress sign, a required personal protective equipment poster. There are many different Visual Information examples. Delineation aisle striping or painting is a form of visual information category (Visual Factory).

- Visual Management Tools: Effective Visual Management is not just for information purposes but is a Management Tool. The tool outlines performance expectations, current state performance, abnormalities to current state performance expectations, and corrective actions status to abnormalities in order to return to current state performance expectations as rapidly as possible. This type of Visual Management can be presented in several formats, to include physical Safety, Quality, Delivery, & Cost Visual Management Boards on the manufacturing floor, electronic counting boards comparing actual performance to required performance, systems that send abnormalities alerts to responsible parties or departments.

Three types of performance indicators

- Lagging Indicators are key performance indicators that measure past performance. The Profit & Loss Statement (Income Statement) is a form of lagging Indicator reporting, measuring the months´ close financial performance.

- Leading Indicators are Key performance indicators that look ahead and attempt to predict future outcomes. They may be contributors to lagging Indicators. For example, the Income Statement as a whole may be a lagging indicator, but some components of the income statement can also be leading indicators. Items such as revenue, or certain variable expenses may predict the year end close results, and demand countermeasure actions if the prediction is not within budgeted limits.

- NOW Indicators are what is occurring real time at the Gemba area. They are typically classified "Green" or "Red". Green indicating that current performance meets or exceeds expectations. Red indicating that an abnormality to the expected performance has occurred and requires as immediate as possible corrective action to return to green status.

All indicators are time sensitive. That is to say that the hour of missed production in the morning was a "NOW" indicator when it happened and required immediate correction or escalation. It later became a "LEADING" indicator at the 2nd level department tier meeting, giving an indication of its possible effect on the day's final results "LAGGING" Indicators.

There is no room for leading and lagging indicators in the Gemba environment where an hour, or minutes or seconds of missed production will affect Delivery and Cost. The only acceptable indicator at Gemba is the NOW indicator. If an abnormality to a Key Performance Indicator expectation occurs, it must be delt with immediately upon discovery. The abnormal condition must be immediately corrected or immediately escalated for correction.

A NOW escalation procedure must be implemented with the 0 tolerance discipline to sustain. This escalation can be achieved using various forms of an Andon. An Andon is a signal that an abnormality has occurred and actions are required (materials, maintenance, etc.). The Andon can be a manual signal actuated by a human, or automatic, such a visible counter, or a computer aided program that automatically sends an alert to an appropriate escalation stakeholder. The process should employ multiple level alerts, each subsequent alert involving a stakeholder to solve the issue. For example, the first alert from an assembly work center may be to the Supervisor. If the first alert issue is not resolved by the Supervisor within a pre-determined time limit, a subsequent alert would be sent to a responsible Manufacturing Engineer, or Maintenance Engineer, depending on the issue and issue severity.

This process will continue until the issue is resolved, or the appropriate escalation stakeholder makes the decision to employ alternate resources which may include external resources. While this escalation process differs from organization to organization, what matters is that the abnormality:

- Has visibility
- It is expeditiously escalated
- It is expeditiously resolved
- The resolution has been incorporated into standard work to prevent recurrence

Shown below is a 1st level cell board illustration showing the NOW indicators and escalation. This can be a manual format or an electronic type format. It is crucial that the chosen format is readily visible, and both root cause & short term countermeasures (Hour x Hour Format and Escalation Process) and Permanent countermeasures are present and visible. A good rule for Visual Management is that someone unfamiliar with the process can quickly understand the current business state.

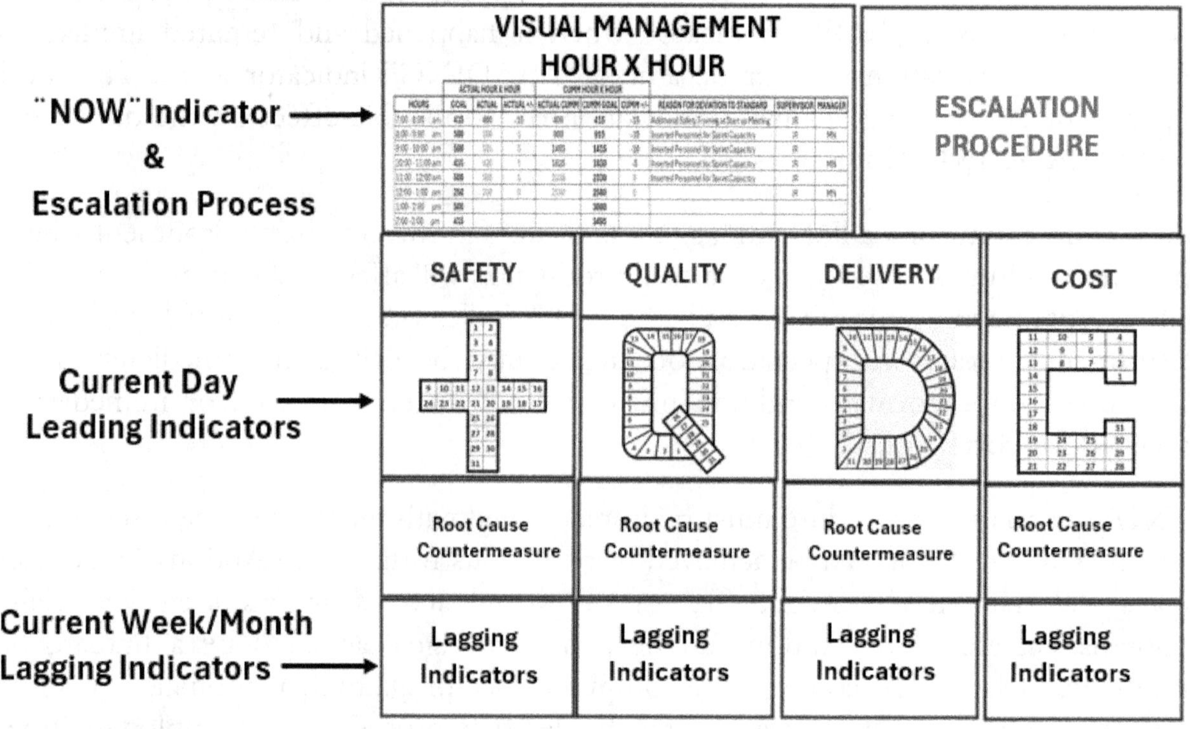

NOW indicators differs from organization to organization. But at a minimum it should cover the areas of Safety, Quality, Delivery, and Cost. Inventory (or working capital) and Personnel (training, engagement, satisfaction, morale) may be covered at level 1 boards or another appropriate Gemba area, or another level in the organization hierarchy.

Organizations do prioritize the above areas differently, and may add or delete an item, but Safety should always be the number one priority of any organization. How an organization defines their expectations, tracks or pulses results, escalates abnormalities to expectations, performs abnormality root cause and corrective actions, will differ, but must occur to achieve and sustain Gemba stability.

Accountability at Gemba

All Gemba NOW Indicators must have an accountable owner. The accountable owner is the person responsible to ensure that compliance to the indicator is achieved and appropriately tracked against the goal, and that escalation and resolution is launched if an actual abnormality versus goal occurs.

Example of a manufacturing Gemba Escalation Hierarchy:

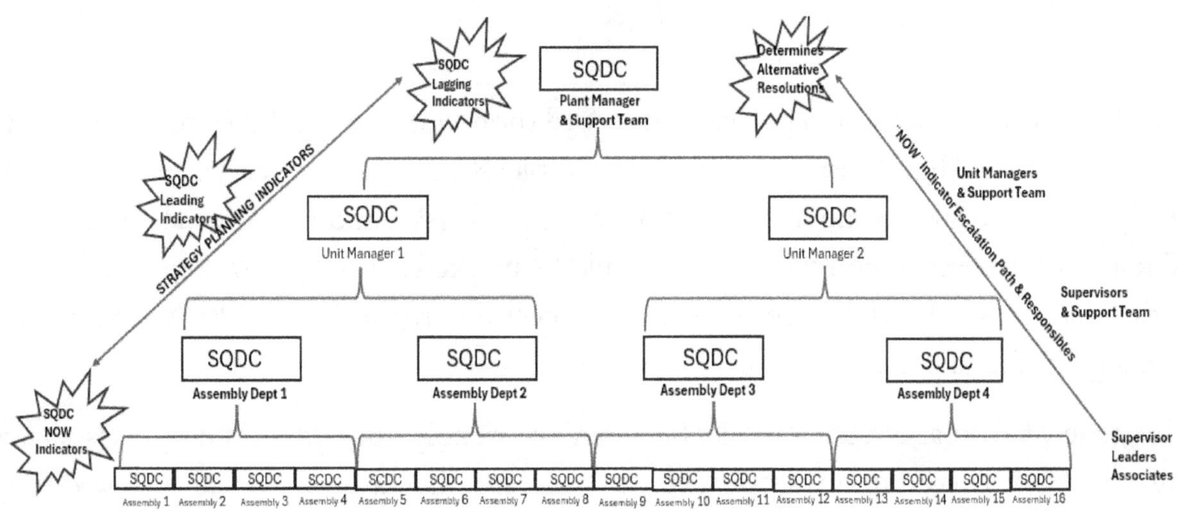

There are multiple methods and formats to assign, track and record accountability assignments. Show below are two examples of Gemba issues assignment & tracking formats.

Rapid Response: Useful for Gemba tasks assignments at Level 1 Safety, Quality, Delivery, & Cost Boards. This type of task assignment and tracking can be integrated as part of the level 1 board. It can be used not only for abnormality issues, but for anything that the area personnel may need to optimally perform their standard work, or to improve the cell equipment or process.

DATE	ISSUE	RESOLUTION	RESPONSIBLE	DATE TO RESOLVE	DATE RESOLVED	STATUS
						⊕
						⊕
						⊕
						⊕
						⊕
						⊕
						⊕
						⊕
						⊕
						⊕

This format would serve as a permanent record (non-erasable), and different pen colors may be used for High Priority items. For example: Red for Safety/Environmental task, designating a priority number 1. Green for 5S related tasks, and Black for all other tasks. When a task is verified complete, a line would be marked across that task on the format. If the task is completed, but verified as not successful, the task could be left open with a change in the "Date to be resolved".

This type of format is very Visual Management friendly and aids to engage associates into the Gemba continuous improvement process. Also, a quick visual review during the Gemba Methodology and Management Gemba Walk processes allows Gemba Walk team members a better understanding of how the downstream Gemba Methodology accountability is functioning.

Accountability Board: A very visible and useful tool for tasks assignments at all tier levels. This type of format is also helpful for organizations struggling with Gemba tasks assignment and completion tracking.

DEPARTMENT____________ MONTH:____________ TEAM LEADER:____________

TEAM	WEEK 1							WEEK 2							WEEK 3						
	1	2	3	4	5	6	7	1	2	3	4	5	6	7	1	2	3	4	5	6	7
Team Member 1		Task								Task											
Team Member 2					Task																
Team Member 3			Task																		
Team Member 4																					
Team Member 5	Task	Task							Task												
Team Member 6					Task																

TASKS COMPLETION RECORD

Tasks can be assigned at the normal daily management tier meetings and recorded on a sticky note or other appropriate medium. As the board is reviewed daily, the Task Owner will provide an update for the assigned task that is scheduled to be completed on that particular day of the week.

When tasks are completed, they are removed from the board to the "Tasks Completion Record".

There are many different types of Visual Management formats, both manual and electronic. Some important concepts of Visual Management Formats:

- Visual Information Only Formats should always be current and updated. If there is an information expiration date, outdated information should be removed. Also, information and boards not being used should be removed. Visual Information provides direction or instruction and must be adhered to, or associates will start to become desensitized to all Visual Information.

- Visual Management Tools are Gemba stability and improvement tools, not just for record keeping. They are used to manage both compliance or non-compliance to expectations, and to launch improvement initiatives. Visual Management Tools that are not being used should also be removed.

Operational Standards at Gemba

Operation Standards at Gemba are a ***Must Have***. Operation Standards are documents (paper or electronic) describing how value added work is to be performed. The Operation Standards may be the derivative of Customer Specifications, Product Design, Manufacturing Process Design, Customer and Internal Quality Standards or a Control Plan.

A particular Gemba environment may already have variables such as absenteeism, rotation, and changes in shifts to deal with. Operation Standards are a key contributor to Gemba stability because they provide consistent instruction to associates on how to perform their value added tasks regardless of personnel variables. Operation Standards provide clear instruction and measurable Safety, Quality and Cost attributes that are used in NOW, Leading, and Lagging indicators. Can you imagine a factory with no Operation Standards, each operator possibly completing value added tasks in a different process sequence, with possible different outcomes.

Operation Standards are the baseline for operational improvements. Standards improvements may come by way of "engaged" associate suggestions, Kaizen activities, Gemba Methodology activities, or problem solving at Gemba. Changes to improve Standards should be verified prior to mass changes. Depending on the complexity of the process, a good verification process is PDCA. Plan-Do-Check-Act (or Adjust). An example of the PDCA methodology is shown below.

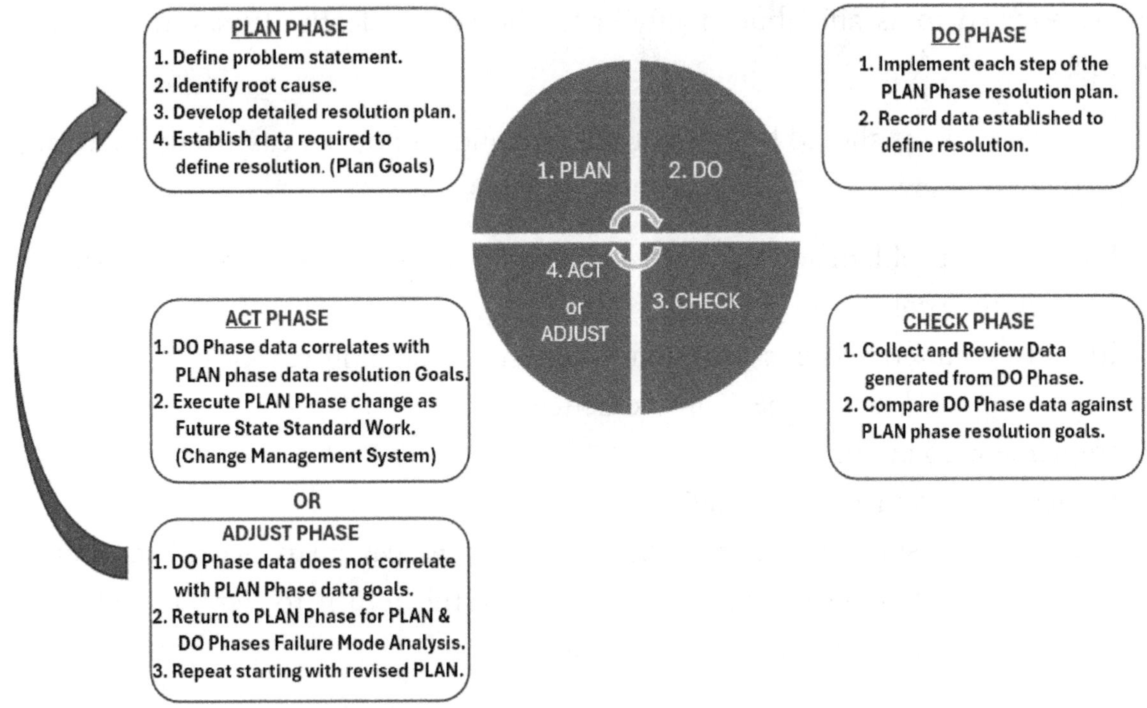

Operation Standards should be periodically audited to ensure that:

- Operators are always following the Operation Standard instruction. (Reference Gemba Methodology Touch Points).
- That the Operation Standard is the correct revision accounting for any changes in the above mentioned documents (Change Management). Companies moving products manufacturing from one facility to another sometimes find out the hard way that Standard Work Instructions and other standards are not current.

If an organization does not have Operations Standards or does not have confidence in the integrity of their current Operation Standards, it is paramount to correct this Gemba Operational Stability Deficiency.

Problem Solving at Gemba

Gemba is referred to as the "Real Place, or the place where value add (and non-value add) tasks are performed. As in any Real Place, there may arise issues that prevent an operation or process from achieving the planned desired results. In Visual Management, this is referred to as an "abnormality" and should be clearly displayed as soon as it occurs.

Resolving problems should be straight forward and somewhat easy to do following the process steps below.

(1) Identify the problem and its effect on planned results. This is a problem statement.
(2) Identify the problem Root Cause.
(3) Identify countermeasures (corrective actions), including responsible personnel to implement, and timeframe of implementation.
(4) Implement countermeasures.
(5) Review countermeasures results.
(6) If countermeasures are successful, use change management to revise operational standards. If countermeasures are not successful, return to item 1. Failure mode analysis for items 1 and 2 may be necessary.

There are several problem solving methodologies to help determine root cause. Below are examples of methodologies that are easy to use in the Gemba setting. Six Sigma methodology offers more advanced problem solving methods, if required.

Just Do It.

This is when the Root Cause is so evident that one does not need to go further. Implement countermeasures and revise operational standards, if applicable. The "Just Do It" process can also be applicable for 'rapid implementation' Improvements.

5 Whys Methodology.

5 Whys is a simple and fast problem solving methodology. It starts with the Problem Statement and works backward to find root cause. Investigating a 1st Why Cause for the Problem Statement, then a Why for the 1st Why and continues until the final consecutive Why questions discover the Root Cause. It may not require all 5 why's to determine root cause or may require more than 5. But the last possible Why is normally considered as the investigation root cause.

As with all problem solving, it is better to work in a team brainstorming environment with personnel that are close to the issue and with subject matter experts if required.

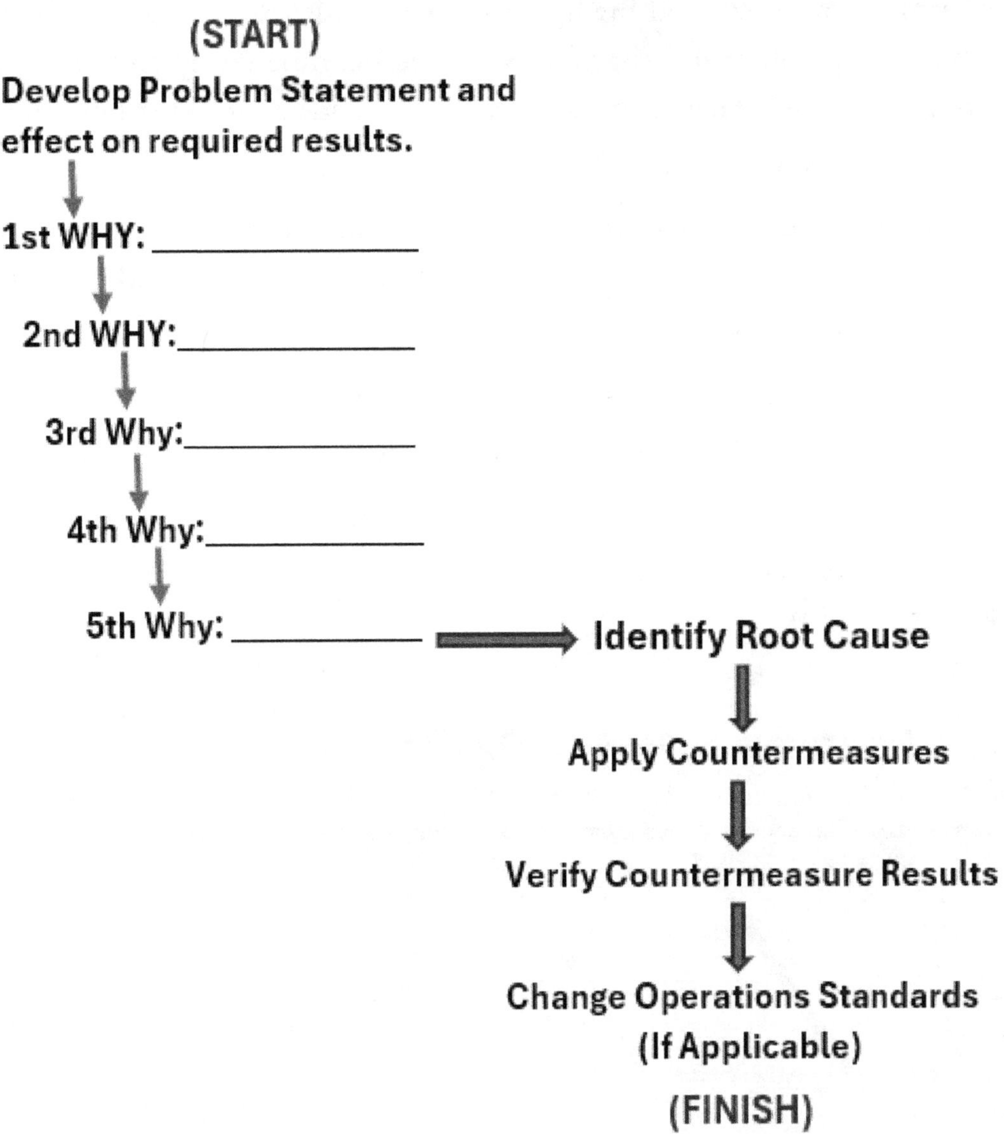

Ishikawa Diagram, (Fishbone), (Cause and Effect Diagram)

The Ishikawa Diagram is another methodology to help identify root cause. Reference the Ishikawa Diagram illustration below. Again, identifying the Problem (or defect) and its effect on required results is the first step. Next is identifying Main Cause categories as shown by the wide lines. The Main Cause categories can be different than those shown, based on the business and the business problem statement.

Next, use a team environment and brainstorm the Potential Root Cause as shown by the narrow lines. The Potential Root Causes can be determined by employing the 5 Why methodology for each Main Cause Category, or the ideas from the brainstorming group.

When the team has exhausted the exercise for determining Potential Root Causes, The team will select the most relevant Root Cause(s) responsible for the problem. This may lead to more than one Root Cause.

Upon identification of Root Cause(s), the team will develop the countermeasures, responsibles to implement, and timeline to implement.

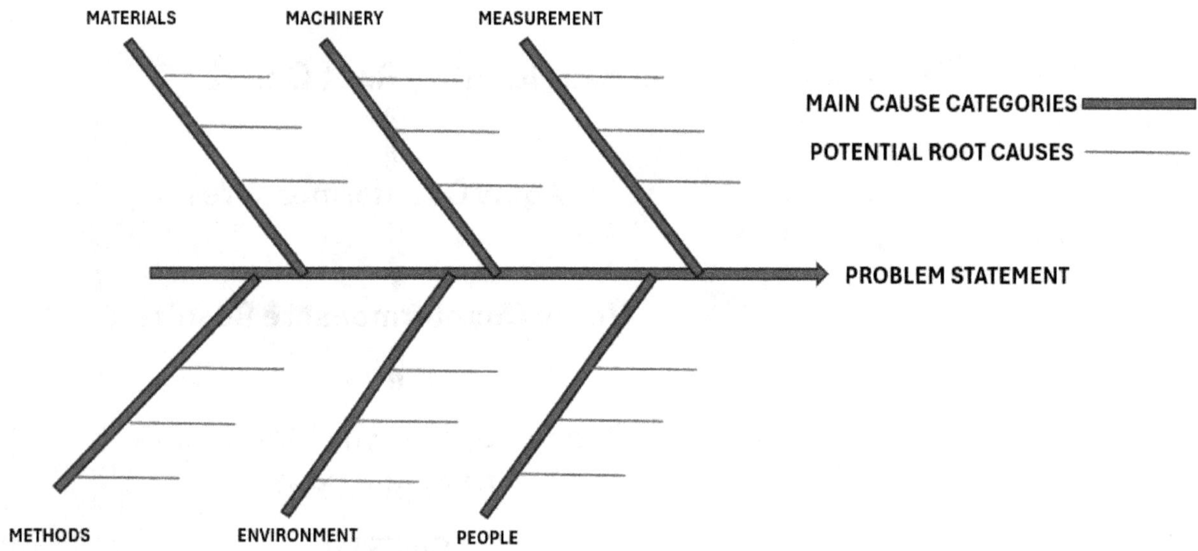

The team brainstorming is more effective if lead by a trained facilitator, such as a graduate from the Circular Training process discussed in the Management Tools & Culture unit. Also, the team brainstorming concept is an excellent method to solicit associate engagement, and to continually train associates in the use of Gemba tools.

Associate Training At Gemba

Lean Training for all associates was discussed In the Management Tools and Culture Unit. Lean training will be essential for all associates involved in the five Lean Business

System Building Blocks transformation. For the associates performing Value Add activities at Gemba, process operations training in accordance with Standardized Work Instruction is also essential to ensure that associates understand and can demonstrate the skill required per the Standardized Work Instructions.

A Visual Gemba Skills Matrix (Training Matrix) is a contributor in many ways to the Gemba Stabilization Culture Transformation. Some of those contributions are shown below.

- Quality at Gemba. A well planned and maintained skills matrix aids to ensure that associates are qualified to perform Standardized Work activities. Also, this process is normally required in many internal and 3rd Party Quality Systems Certification Programs.
- Associate Teambuilding. A current and properly maintained Skills Matrix promotes teambuilding at Gemba. Associates can see their contribution to their Gemba Team.
- Associate Engagement/Satisfaction. When the Skills Matrix is a contributor to job classifications and compensation, associates can visualize a path to progression within the organization.
- Production Planning & Productivity Optimization. Lean and Skills trained associates are better equipped to safely produce quality products per Standardized Work Instructions within the designed flow Cycle Time. Production Planning is able to level load the production floor with a higher degree of confidence as Gemba stability gets traction.

An example of a Gemba Value Add Skills Matrix is shown below.

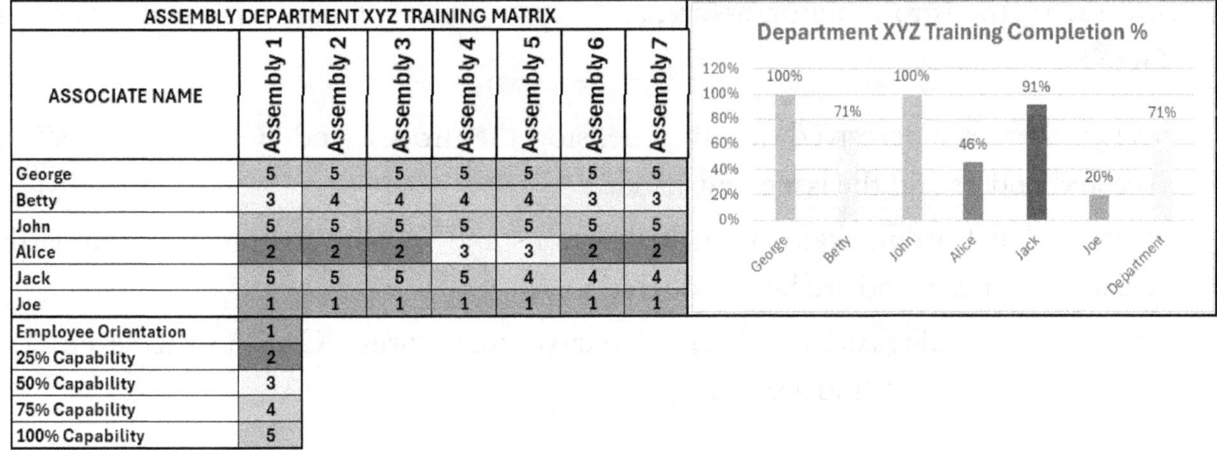

ASSEMBLY DEPARTMENT XYZ TRAINING MATRIX							
ASSOCIATE NAME	Assembly 1	Assembly 2	Assembly 3	Assembly 4	Assembly 5	Assembly 6	Assembly 7
George	5	5	5	5	5	5	5
Betty	3	4	4	4	4	3	3
John	5	5	5	5	5	5	5
Alice	2	2	2	3	3	2	2
Jack	5	5	5	5	4	4	4
Joe	1	1	1	1	1	1	1

Employee Orientation	1
25% Capability	2
50% Capability	3
75% Capability	4
100% Capability	5

A Skills Matrix can be designed using various formats and can be utilized in any area of an organization where processes are being performed, either on the manufacturing floor or administrative processes. An important aspect of the Skills Matrix Process is that it is well planned and accurately maintained. Associates will quickly become disengaged and demoralized if training is not delivered as required, especially if it is linked to job classification and/or compensation.

Process and Product Quality In Gemba Culture

Gemba Methodology is all about Stabilizing Business Performance where the Value Add activities are being performed. The Lean Business System Quality Assurance topic is segregated into Gemba Tools and Culture, and Kaizen Tools and Culture.

- Gemba Quality Assurance: Ensuring that Current State Quality Assurance tools & processes are being used and are effective.
- Kaizen Quality Assurance: Improving upon the Current State Quality Assurance tools & processes.

Nothing is more disappointing or demoralizing than having a process or product quality escape because a Quality Assurance tool or process was not adhered to. Upon investigation, the organization learns that there is a process in place and "we used to do it". Following the Lean Business System building blocks example, the organization should ensure that the current state Quality Assurance Tools and Processes are being effectively utilized.

Below are methods to monitor, assure, and improve current state tools and processes at Gemba.

- When there is a perceived quality issue, stop the process and "Go To Gemba" to see and understand the issue first-hand.
- Ensure that Current State Work Instructions and Quality Instructions Standards exist, are current, and are being adhered to.
- Ensure that Quality Assurance gages, poka-yokes, fixtures, SCADA systems, etc. are in place, being used, and are effective.

- Ensure that all associates are empowered to stop operations in the event of a perceived Safety or Quality issue. Employ the mantra of "Stop, Escalate, Wait".
- Ensure that a Skills Matrix type training program is being utilized, is effective, and is current.
- Employ start of shift and intermittent Safety and Quality processes check lists.
- Use the Gemba Methodology to employ Process and Quality engineers/personnel to use critical process and quality 'Touch Points' as part of their Gemba Methodology Daily Tasks.
- Employ associate "Quality Circles" engagement for Preventative initiatives and Post Incident investigations.
- Use Productivity Systems such as Daily Management and Overall Equipment Effectiveness (OEE) Quality Data for Problem Solving quality improvements.
- Use Gemba Methodology and Management Gemba Walking as a method to engage associates regarding Safety and Quality topics.

Materials Stability at Gemba

One of the items discussed in the Management Tools & Culture was the prevention of organizational silos. While Materials Management may be thought of as a different science than Operations, nevertheless, their Customer is Gemba. Their performance metrics should not only be lowest landed cost, but should be 'Leading' indicator metrics linked directly to the success of Gemba.

The organization´s Materials Resource Planning set-up (master) data should be configured to support Gemba. Stakeholders such as Customers, Associates, and Shareholders will remain unsatisfied if Gemba is not stable and meeting Strategy planning expectations.

While Operations and Supply Chain may occupy different accounts on the Profit & Loss Statement, it is organizational top echelon management's responsibility to not allow siloing of metrics that damage the overall Gemba performance, and thus the overall Profit & Loss performance.

Accountable Materials Management or Sourcing personnel should be present at Gemba floor tier meetings. Supply Chain 'NOW' or 'Leading' indicators that negatively affect

Gemba performance should be immediately investigated for root cause and permanent countermeasure corrective action(s). Corrective action(s) should also be investigated for possible replication across the entire Enterprise Resource Planning and/or Materials Requirements Planning systems.

Materials Management will also normally encompass Maintenance, Repair, and Operating materials and supplies (MRO). The discussion above regarding Supply Chain ERP/MRP data configuration, 'NOW' and 'Leading' indicators, also applies to MRO management.

Think of it as building a world class vehicle that cannot perform due to lack of fuel. The fuel supplier is a servant to the requirements of the vehicle, and so it is with Materials Management and Gemba.

Sense of Urgency at Gemba

Work with a Sense of Urgency, Be Proactive – Not Reactive.

The Sense of Urgency Skill may seem like a soft skill, or something not easy to describe, like the "force" in a Star Wars movie. But Sense of Urgency is a necessary hard skill and is incredibly important regarding Gemba. As discussed earlier in this unit, time resolution at Gemba is in seconds or fractions of a second, so the ability to recognize degrees of urgency and take appropriate expeditionary corrective actions are of utmost importance.

While the Sense of Urgency is required across all business disciplines, it is at Gemba where a lack of Sense of Urgency can manifest in immediate damage to "Now" indicators. Appropriate Sense of Urgency must be demonstrated by all management personnel. Again, what is not important to management will not be important to the rest of the organization.

Appropriate Sense of Urgency is also important, that is to say that an emergency is urgent, but not every urgency is an emergency. Abnormalities to "Now" indicators must be immediately visible and recognized by assigned responsible personnel, so that decisive, immediate, and appropriate "sense of urgency" corrective actions can be implemented. The goal should be to recover any Daily Management deficiency caused from the abnormality to prevent 'Leading' indicator damage.

A Gemba urgency will still exist and negatively affect performance even if it is not recognized. If an organization detects that assigned key personnel do not possess an adequate Sense of Urgency skill, then additional training should be implemented. This selected training can also be added to the training regime discussed in the "Management Tools and Culture" unit.

Associate respect, engagement, and empowerment at Gemba.

It is important to keep reminding oneself that the Gemba Culture Building Block is about stabilization and plugging the holes in the Gemba wastes leaky bucket. To gain Gemba stability, a critical step in the journey is to begin turning the organizational hierarchy from controlling to supporting. This requires daily attentiveness to the Gemba Tools and Culture basics, and to the associates performing those basics.

- Management Engagement: Management must be Gemba trained and understand their role in the Gemba Methodology. Consistent and active engagement at the Gemba level is required to support implementation and sustainability of the Gemba basics. Lack of Gemba engagement by any of the organization's management team members will jeopardize Gemba stability and therefore jeopardize stakeholder's satisfaction. Like it or not, organizational management is always being watched and judged regarding their Gemba engagement. At the risk of using an already overused cliché, managers must "Walk The Walk".
- Gemba basics training (Gemba 101) is necessary as soon as possible. All associates must understand the tools that make Gemba stability possible.
- Striving for associate empowerment is key. This begins with Safety and Quality. Associates must be able to:
  - Recognize abnormalities to Safety & Quality Standards.
  - Be able to stop an operation or process if a "perceived" abnormality occurs.
  - Escalate and wait for the appropriate organization support to assess and resolve the issue.
- Development of High Performance Teams. There should be no silos in Gemba management. Everyone has a contributing role to Gemba Methodology, and everyone should show respect and support to each other's Gemba role, and their expertise required to perform that role.

- There must be standardization at Gemba. Operational Standards are the foundation of Gemba stabilization. If Operational Standards are weak or non-existent, expeditious correction is necessary.
- Practice consistent discipline regarding 5S/6S, waste elimination, visual management, and accountability at Gemba.
- Demonstrated "sense of urgency" when abnormalities threaten Gemba stability. Complacency has no place in the Gemba culture.

Burn the Boats - Enjoy the Journey

UNIT 3 - KAIZEN TOOLS & CULTURE

Relentless Business Performance Improvements

A Review of Management & Gemba Cultures

The Management Culture involved a new way of professional thinking and managing the business. Managers now are better Lean Business System trained. They are transitioning from their previous controlling role to a supporting role; they have developed their Leader Standard Work; they are using the Safety-Quality-Delivery-Cost compass to manage issues; and they are consistently engaged at Gemba to promote associate training, teamwork, and the Gemba stability basics.

The Gemba Culture focused on improving the stabilization of Gemba. Associates have a better understanding of Value Add tasks vs Non-value Add tasks and they now can identify wastes at Gemba. The organization is implementing a Gemba Methodology process; a sustainable 5S/6S Methodology; Visual Management & Accountability; and basic Problem Solving processes at Gemba. Operational Standards are being reviewed, and associates are becoming more empowered and engaged regarding Safety and Quality.

Adding the Kaizen Tools and Culture

According to the Oxford Advanced American Dictionary.

"kaizen is a Japanese word that means "continuous improvement". It is a business term that refers to the practice of constantly improving a company's operations".

The Kaizen Continuous Business Improvement Culture is the core value in the never ending pursuit of perfection. Kaizen Culture should touch and permeate all organizational business disciplines, because wastes does exist everywhere in the business.

Now that the foundations of Management Culture and Gemba Culture have been laid and are getting traction, it's time to start laying on real and sustainable business improvements. The Kaizen Culture will focus on tools and cultural change to drive consistent and sustainable business improvements across the organization. Improvements that have measurable positive impact to the Profit & Loss.

Before embarking on the Kaizen Tools & Culture Unit, it may be worthwhile to review again the Lean Business System Cultures Roadmap.

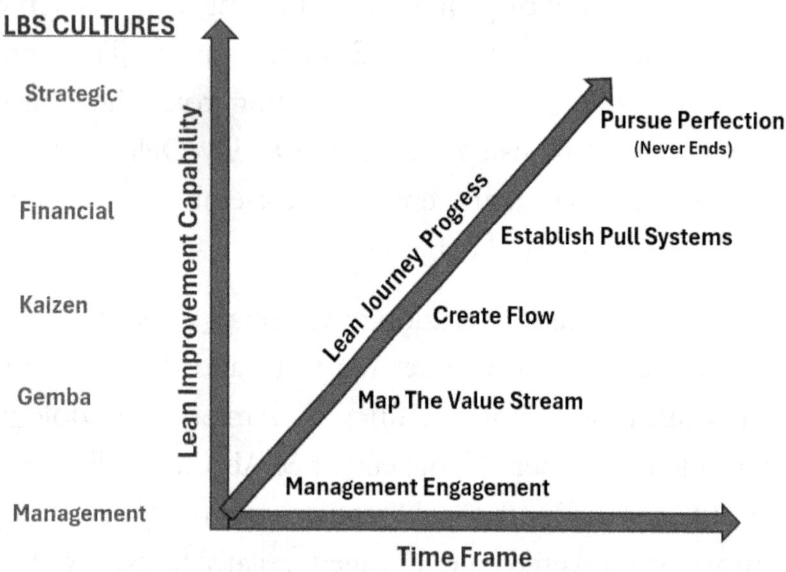

The Lean Business System Cultures Roadmap suggests several Lean Tools that can be used to improve Safety, Quality, Delivery, & Cost, and to improve associate engagement & stakeholders satisfaction. But within the Lean Business System Methodology there are also several other methods to drive business improvements. These may include employee's suggestions, Income Statement analysis, Supply Chain improvements, and process improvements across all business disciplines, to include administrative back office. This unit highlights the importance of relentless Lean Methodology waste reduction across the organization and is a major input to the Site Improvement Planning tools in the Financial and Strategy Lean Business System building blocks.

Kaizen Waste Reduction Tools

(1) Cost of Poor Quality (COPQ)

The Gemba Tools and Culture unit reviewed the eight wastes that associates should be able to recognize in order to eliminate the Hidden Factory. But Defects waste is just the tip of the Income Statement iceberg when referring to the Cost of Poor Quality. There is nothing that can erode an organization's Profit and Loss so quickly, so unexpectedly, and so dramatically as issues relating to poor quality. It is easy to recant the calculation for Cost Of Poor Quality or display PowerPoint presentations showing the COPQ effects of scrap, sorting, rework, and warranty claims. But within the Gemba and Kaizen Cultures building blocks, the sustainable preventative reduction/elimination of these COPQ components should be of top priority since each of these components can cause significant damage to the organization's Profit and Loss. An event of the worst case Products Quality Recall could cause an organization severe financial stress, or even create a bankrupt situation. Below is an example of how unanticipated COPQ components can negatively affect many individual accounts within an organization's monthly financial Income Statement versus their budgeted Profit & Loss.

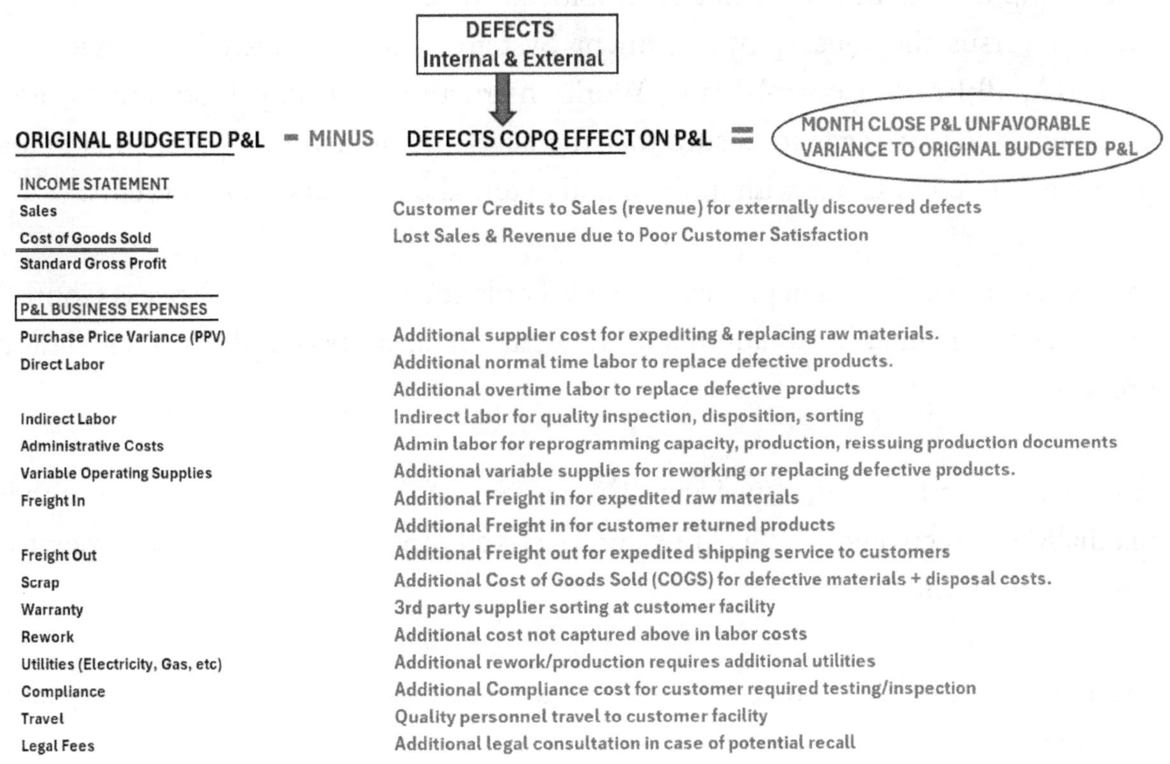

If the bad news is the possible devastating consequences of Cost Of Poor Quality, the good news is that there are preventative processes and post-issue countermeasures that can significantly reduce the Profit & Loss wastes due to Cost Of Poor Quality.

In the Gemba Tools & Culture, the section "Quality at Gemba" discussed methods to assure that current state quality assurance tools and processes are being utilized and are effective.

In the Kaizen Tools and Culture, additional quality improvements can be layered on the Gemba Tools and Culture quality measures already in place, as shown below.

- The organization's Quality Management System (QMS) should be designed to ensure that manufacturing and quality processes produce products that meet all internal and external safety and quality requirements. A regular review of the QMS should be conducted to ensure that all internal and external stakeholder's requirements are adequately included.

- Kaizen activity (Kaizen Events) can be structured to focus on Quality Assurance. For example, a Kaizen team can be employed to review the actual manufacturing process versus the Quality Management System. This may include a review of DFEMA, PFEMA, Control Plans, Work Instructions, Quality Instructions, and associated tools & gages to ensure that the actual manufacturing practice is being performed in compliance with internal and external customers' requirements.

- Implementing additional in process Quality Tools such as Statistical Process Control (SPC) either manually or automatically with an appropriate Andon escalation process.

- Ensuring that processes, especially "Critical Specifications" processes, are either manually or electronically (SCADA) poka yoked, and not reliant upon operator pass/fail decision.

- Employ process Data Acquisition systems wherever possible for improved quality data analysis, and improvement opportunities.

- Periodic 3rd party review of Quality Systems Compliance. This is not a certification audit, but a Subject Matter Expert walking the process for quality compliance verification, and for Quality Assurance improvement suggestions.

- Additional training in industry standard Quality Assurance Core Tools for key personnel, or all personnel if possible.

(2) Gemba Wastes Reduction.

As the Gemba Culture starts to gain traction, the Safety, Quality, Delivery & Cost improvements should become increasingly evident, depending on where the organization's Lean Business System journey started from. It may be difficult to capture every stabilization improvement that results from improved engagement initiatives such as Waste Identification & Elimination, 5S/6S, and Visual Management, but with individual work cell tier level management, the Safety, Quality, Delivery and Cost improvements should be visible and should be reflected in the Profit & Loss in the form of quality and productivity improvements. Some of those Profit & Loss improvements are detailed below.

- Safety: Every first aid, near miss, or accident comes with a cost in either medical services, workers compensation, medical insurance, employee absenteeism, rotation, or negative morale. A Safety First, 0 tolerance, Safety & Health program, including employee empowerment & training, 5S/6S standards, ergonomics, and employee welfare is necessary for positive employee engagement and favorable translation to the Profit & Loss Statement.

- Quality: The unfavorable effects of Cost of Poor Quality to the Profit & Loss were discussed above. But continual quality issues not only cost money, but will erode the confidence of customers, and is a display to employees that management is not adequately engaged.

- Delivery: Poor Internal and external customer delivery can create addition costs for overtime labor, expedited logistics cost to customers, and possibly lost sales and revenue due to eroded customer confidence. Gemba Methodology, Gemba Wastes

Elimination, and Tier Level "NOW" indicators Visual Management should have a positive effect on both internal and external customer delivery.

- Cost: As the Gemba Tools and Culture building blocks efforts gain engagement traction, the cost contributor of increased labor productivity should see a corresponding favorable Profit & Loss gain.

The organization should develop Safety, Quality, Delivery, & Cost "Leading" Gemba Profit & Loss, and employee engagement key indicators to track the progress of both during the Gemba Tools and Culture Building Block ramp-up phase.

(3) Associate's Ideas.

Nothing is more satisfying to associates and to management than when associates are engaged in developing and presenting improvement ideas, especially when these innovative ideas become reality. An employee Ideas program is a great way to drive the Gemba and Kaizen associate engagement, and to generate potential waste/cost reduction projects for the organization's Site Improvement Planning Funnel.

There are items to consider before embarking on this type of program in order to achieve optimal associate engagement and program sustainability.

- The more Gemba and Kaizen training that employees receive, the better equipped they are to identify and describe feasible improvement ideas. Management should program the Lean/Gemba Training discussed in the Management Tools and Culture Unit as preparation for the associate's improvement ideas campaign.

- The guidelines of the program should be clear and well communicated to associates to avoid confusion once the program is in place.

- There should be suggestion program boundaries to keep associates focused on the organization's main pains, and ensure that suggestions feasibility are realistic.

- Employees should have an opportunity to present their ideas to a review team, ideally represented by a mix of peers, management, and appropriate support administration. This should be a planned periodic review, and employees advised in advance when their suggestion is on the review agenda. A standardized suggestion presentation format works well, and presentation preparation help is a good idea, especially for first time presenters. If all ideas cannot be presented, all ideas should be recognized. An organization Associates Suggestions Board displayed in a heavy foot traffic area is great for engagement and morale.

- An important item to consider is that this type of program requires administration. Ideas need to be formally registered and recognized. They need to be reviewed for effort/benefit feasibility before just dumping into the Site Improvement Planning Funnel. Employee presentations, recognition, and rewards require organization and planning. The organization needs to ensure appropriate resources are dedicated to maintain program sustainability.

- The program should never be allowed to become a "window dressing program". The Associates Continuous Improvement Ideas Program should be a foundation program for Kaizen Culture success. Ideas recognition, formally or informally, is paramount for associate engagement and participation in the Kaizen Culture phase. Suggestions that are feasibility selected for insertion into the Site Improvement Program funnel are a win/win for all business stakeholders.

(4) Profit & Loss (Income Statement) Variations

With appropriate Daily Management at all organizational levels and disciplines. Managers responsible for Profit & Loss account balances should not be surprised by unexpected large variations against their Profit & Loss budgeted forecasts. Some Profit & Loss formats can be quite involved based on the complexity of the business, so some ground rules should apply as below.

- Managers should understand well and be accountable for their Profit & Loss accounts responsibility. They should understand what credits and debits are inputs to their responsible accounts, and how to make input adjustments if necessary (referred to as ´pulling the levers´). Daily Management of 'Now' and 'Leading indicators' allows for immediate implementation of adjustment countermeasures.

- Continuous Improvement personnel, working with Finance, should understand the organization's Profit & Loss format and mine the data for improvement opportunities.

- The organization Finance Head should be equally responsible for actual Profit & Loss variations versus budgeted forecasts. The Finance Head should be the clearing house for budget forecasts, validating accounts forecasts with the accounts owners. The Finance Head should ensure that Profit & Loss account owners are: (1) adequately Profit & Loss educated (2) not allowed to submit budget forecasts that are not supported by either reasonable historic trends and/or reasonable future business events changes.

- Significant unexpected account variations (favorable or unfavorable) should be explored for root cause and corrective actions. Continual improvement of forecast accuracy is another contributor to the Lean Business System Methodology.

- The "Red is Red and Green is Red" philosophy is a reminder that just because an expense may be budgeted, does not mean there is not opportunity for further improvement.
  - Accounts that are constantly favorable should be adjusted for improved forecast accuracy.
  - Variable expense accounts that, although budgeted, exceed industry best practice expectations should be reviewed for savings opportunities. Examples may be Direct or indirect labor, scrap, rework, variable supplies, etc.
  - Fixed expense accounts may generally be considered untouchable, but opportunities for renegotiation or reduced usage savings should be explored.

- Cost Accountants should be working as business partners with management and account holders in the relentless pursuit of waste elimination. Cost Accountants may have access to more detailed Profit & Loss data and should use that data to highlight potential waste/cost elimination opportunities.

(5) Value Stream Mapping (VSM)

Value Stream Mapping is an ideal Lean Tool for exposing the hidden factory or inefficient back office processes. It can be applied to any business discipline and is also another great employee engagement promotor. The VSM exercise should involve employees from the area of concentration, from supplier (inputs) and customer (outputs) areas, from information flow areas, as well as other possible subject matter contributors. Value Steam Mapping ideally should be led by a trained and experienced Kaizen Leader. Refer to the Associate Training and Engagement section in the Management Culture Unit for developing Kaizen facilitators.

VSM Kaizen Guideline Steps:

•The Management Team or Continuous Improvement Area or Site Improvement Planning Committee should define the scope of the VSM via a Kaizen Event Charter. Is the scope enterprise wide to include organization suppliers and customers, or plant wide, or process specific.

•Schedule the Kaizen event on the Kaizen Calendar. Give participants and their managers as much advance notice as possible. Chaotic event scheduling will erode participation and engagement.

•Train the Kaizen event participants. It is necessary for the event participants to understand the Kaizen Charter and Value Stream Mapping process. This can be accomplished as a prework meeting or in the event kick off meeting.

•Create a current state Value Stream process map. The team will need to walk the process in order to gather the materials, processes, and information flow required.

•The team should also be conducting a "waste safari" looking for the 8 basic wastes as they are walking the process.

•Use standard Value Stream Mapping process map icons when creating both the current state and future state maps.

•Review the current state map and the waste elimination and process improvement suggestions gathered by the Kaizen Team. Other potential improvement observations such as safety, 5S, excessive work in process inventory, maintenance and quality should also be noted.

•Produce a Value Steam Improvements List. This list contains all the improvements to be captured in the future state map. The improvements list should have quantified improvement values such as materials, processing times, and inventory reductions. These are critical inputs to the Future State Map, and also for input into the Site Improvement Plan Funnel. 'Just Do It' improvements that were completed during the event should also be reported on the Improvements List.

•Create the Future State Map from the VSM Improvements List.

Note: Depending on the Lean maturity of the organization, the Value Stream Mapping methodology can generate many improvement ideas for the Site Improvement Planning Funnel. Due diligence should be exercised to concentrate on critical value streams and selection of Safety, Quality, Delivery, & Cost "main pains" and major Return On Investment projects.

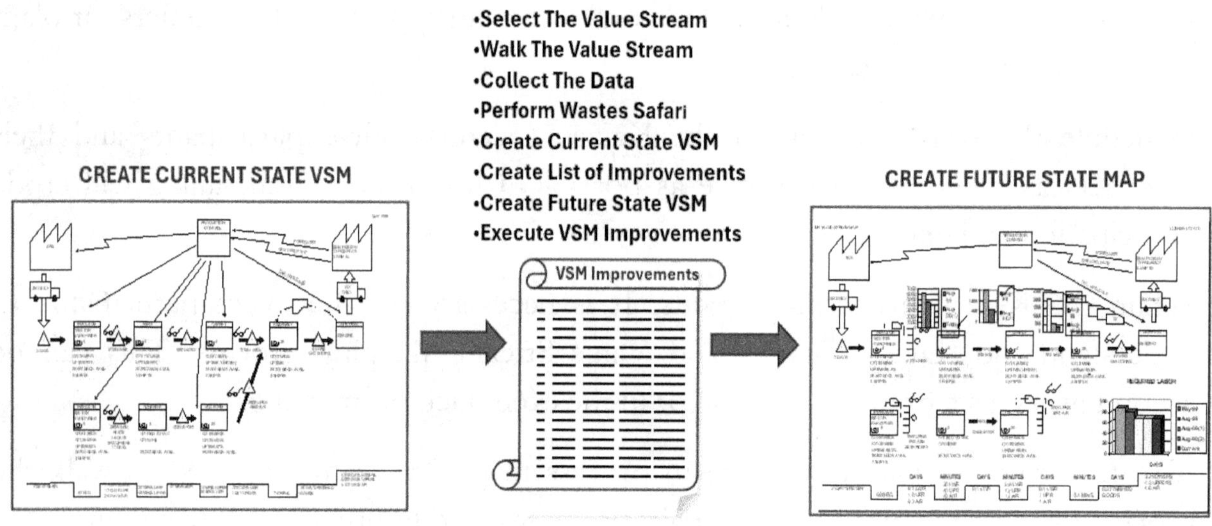

(6) Creating Process Flow (Design for Flow Methodology)

Creating Process Flow is perhaps the most powerful Lean Tool in the Lean Manufacturing Toolbox. This methodology allows the organization to produce products to (1) Highest Quality (2) Shortest Leadtime (3) Lowest Cost. These three performance attributes are exactly what the organization stakeholders are looking for.

This powerful Lean methodology may also be referred to as One-piece Flow, Single piece flow, Continuous Flow, or Line Balancing. The methodology incorporates a variety of Lean Tools such as Takt Time Analysis, Production Level Loading (heijunka), Improved Capacity Planning, Set up Wheel, and Built in Quality.

Beware of the principal hidden factory deficiency of Fake Flow. The Gemba Culture Unit covered how both value add and non-value activity can both be occurring at Gemba. Fake Flow is a great example of non-value activity. There are glaring symptoms of Fake Flow that are easy to spot at Gemba, as described below.

•Batch Production.

•Equipment not arranged in process sequence.

•Work in Process inventory (WIP) in the process line.

•No process cadence to a "Takt" time.

•Low Productivity or Efficiency against design standards.

•Any of the classic eight wastes are also symptoms of interrupted flow.

There is an old adage among trained Lean Practitioners,

"If you can't see flow – there's not flow"

How to Create Flow:

•Select the process area to perform the Flow Kaizen. This selection could be based on volume, productivity, or other Safety, Quality, Delivery, & Cost main pain attributes.

•Understand the Process Routing by doing a Part Process Route Analysis. This analysis can be done by spreadsheet analysis (example below). This analysis will aid to determine which part numbers have similar process routings and can be grouped in the flow design.

PROCESS ROUTE FLOW ANALYSIS-Current State

DEMAND INFORMATION					PROCESS ROUTE INFORMATION						
ITEM	PART NUMBER	DEMAND QTY	CUMM QTY	% of CUMM	OP10	OP20	OP30	30A	OP40	OP50	OP60
1	XYZ001	500	500	23%	1	2	3		4	5	6
2	XYZ002	450	950	43%	1	2	3		4	5	6
3	XYZ003	400	1350	61%	1	2	3		4	5	6
4	XYZ004	300	1650	75%	1	2	3		4	5	6
5	XYZ005	250	1900	**86%**	1	2	3		4	5	6
6	XYZ006	200	2100	95%	1	2		3	4	5	6
7	XYZ007	50	2150	98%	1	2		3	4	5	6
8	XYZ008	50	2200	100%	1	2		3	4	5	6
		2200									

•Perform process time studies for each process on the Part Process Route Analysis.

- Time studies should be separated by Operator Time & Equipment Time.

- Process times should be broken down into individual steps within each process. This data will be used in the future state Yamazumi/Operator Load Chart balancing analysis.

PROCESS ROUTE TIME ANALYSIS-Current State

DEMAND INFORMATION					PROCESS CYCLE TIME INFORMATION						
ITEM	PART NUMBER	DEMAND QTY	CUMM QTY	% of CUMM	OP10	OP20	OP30	30A	OP40	OP50	OP60
1	XYZ001	500	500	23%	55	45	50		45	70	9
2	XYZ002	450	950	43%	55	45	50		45	70	9
3	XYZ003	400	1350	61%	55	45	50		45	70	9
4	XYZ004	300	1650	75%	55	45	50		45	70	9
5	XYZ005	250	1900	**86%**	55	45	50		45	70	9
6	XYZ006	200	2100	95%	55	45		50	45	70	9
7	XYZ007	50	2150	98%	55	45		50	45	70	9
8	XYZ008	50	2200	100%	55	45		50	45	70	9
		2200									

•Perform a Spaghetti Diagram for the current process flow. (example below). This diagram will be used to visualize and reduce/eliminate operator walking and/or transportation, one of the eight basic wastes.

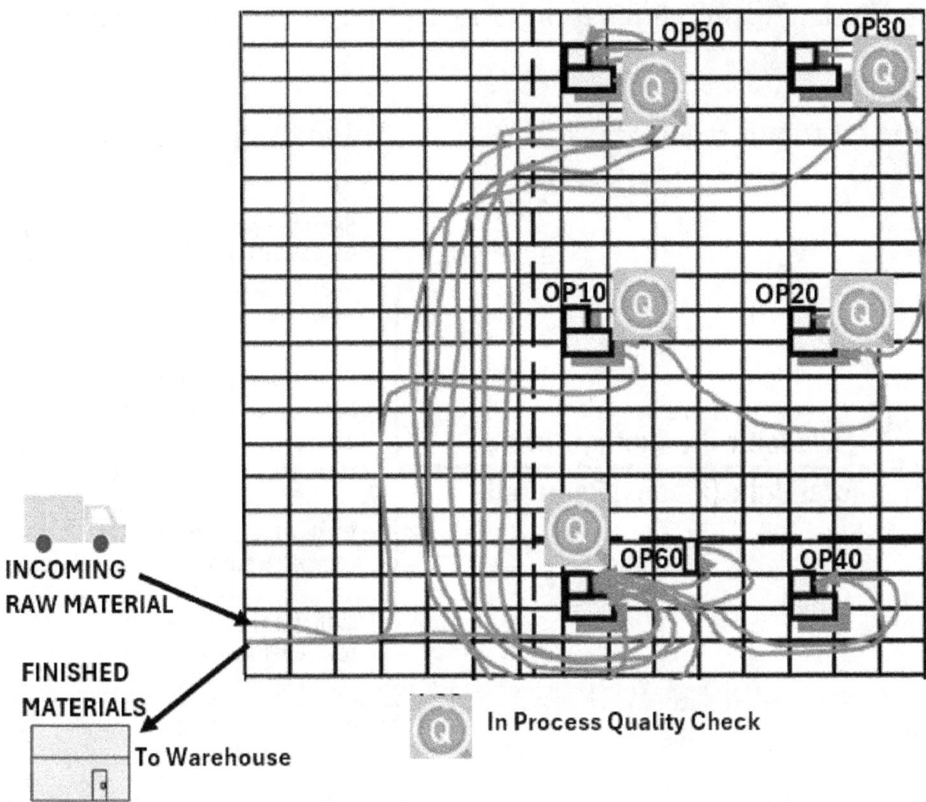

•Create a Current State Kaizen Flow Statistics analysis, to include:

- Total square footage that the current processes layout is occupying.
- Total process lead time (the sum of all process cycle times).
- Headcount.
- Process area productivity.
- Operator walking distance.
- Parts transportation distance.
- Work in process and finished goods inventory.
- Operation changeover times.

This information will also be required for a comparison of Current State design to the Future State design waste elimination, and for a Kaizen report out presentation to management.

•Calculate the customer required takt time. Calculation example below.

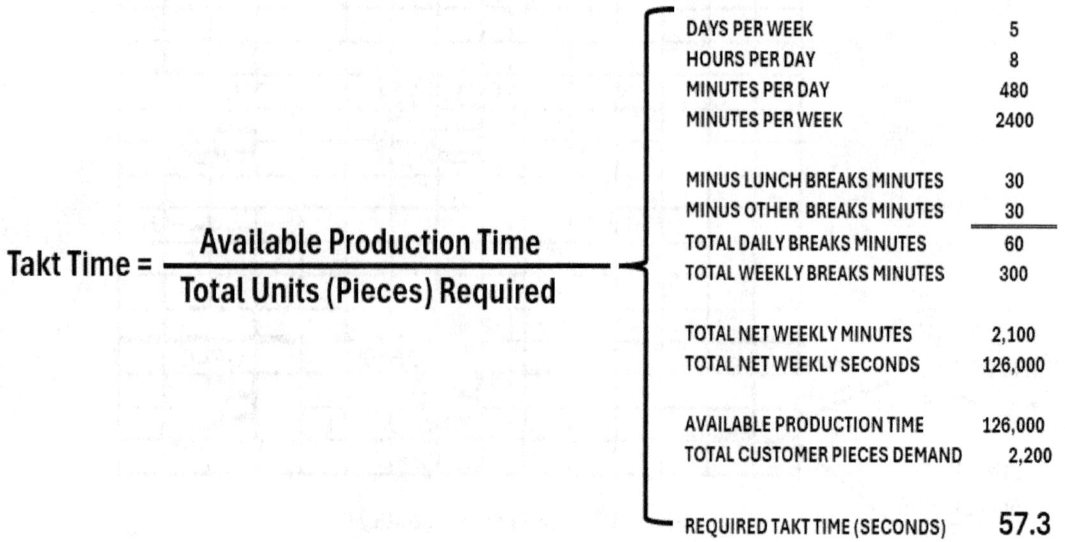

Takt Time = Available Production Time / Total Units (Pieces) Required

DAYS PER WEEK	5
HOURS PER DAY	8
MINUTES PER DAY	480
MINUTES PER WEEK	2400
MINUS LUNCH BREAKS MINUTES	30
MINUS OTHER BREAKS MINUTES	30
TOTAL DAILY BREAKS MINUTES	60
TOTAL WEEKLY BREAKS MINUTES	300
TOTAL NET WEEKLY MINUTES	2,100
TOTAL NET WEEKLY SECONDS	126,000
AVAILABLE PRODUCTION TIME	126,000
TOTAL CUSTOMER PIECES DEMAND	2,200
REQUIRED TAKT TIME (SECONDS)	57.3

•Prepare the draft Operator Load Chart using Takt Time and Cycle Time inputs. The exercise can also display a Yamazumi Chart which is similar to the Load Chart, except it utilizes stacked bar charting to show individual cycle times for each task within an operation, or value add, non-value add, and necessary non-value add times within an operation. This data is collected from the original process time study data and is used to construct the below Operator Load Charts.

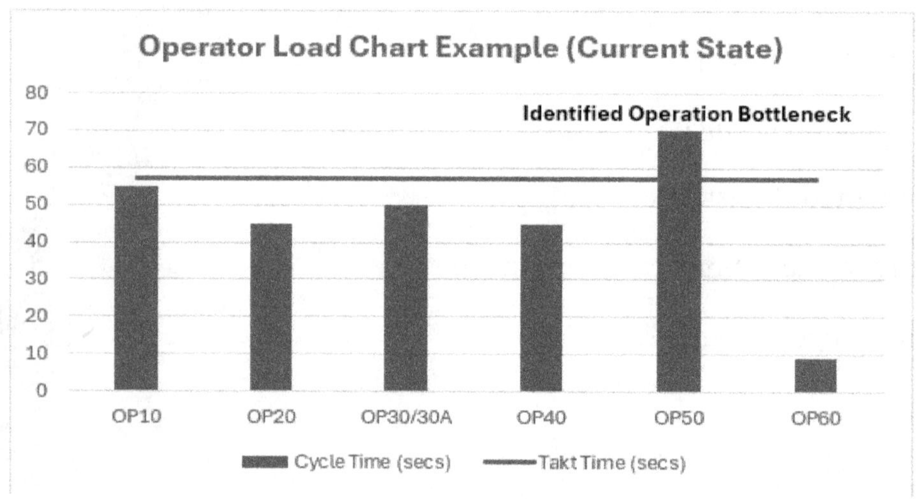

The Current State Operator Load Chart displayed a bottleneck operation. The Kaizen team discovered that the OP50 bottleneck operation must be resolved.

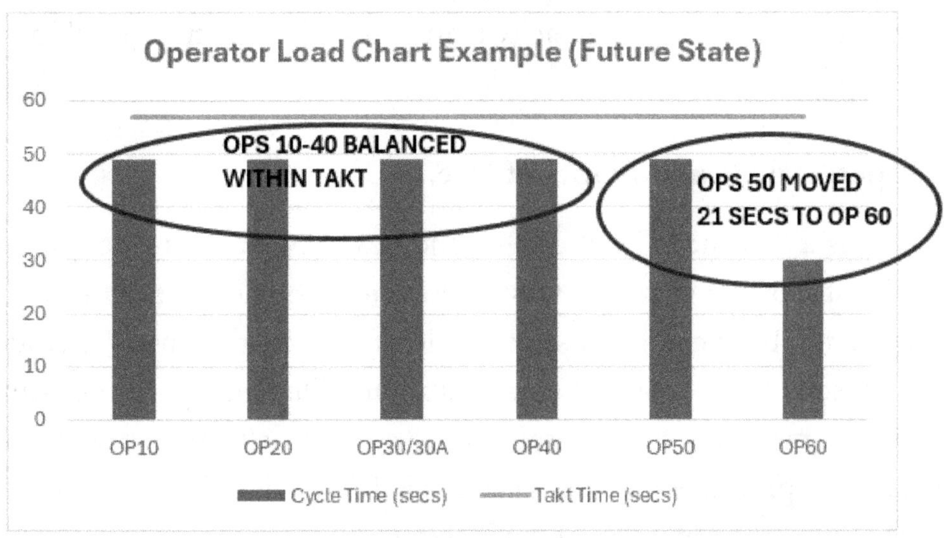

After a draft process line design utilizing data from the individual tasks Yamazumi Chart, the Kaizen team developed a better balanced process cell by distributing individual operation tasks among operators.

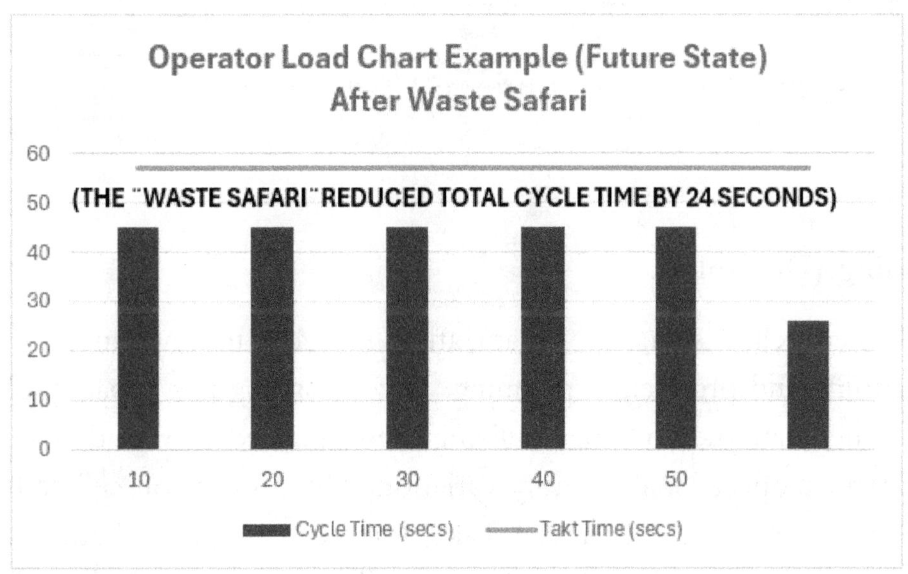

The Kaizen team has also applied processes waste reductions from the Waste Safari that they documented while walking the processes. Using the VA/NVA Yamasumi data, they were able to rebalance the Operator Load Chart and design the new process cell, removing an additional 24 seconds of non-value add activity. This revised cell configuration will facilitate better capacity planning and production level loading.

Materials Supermarkets and Points of Use.

Now that there is a "balanced" cell design, the next key step is to design the process cell material flow to further eliminate waste. Operators should operate. That means they should not leave the balanced process cell to look for components. Operators should always have "close at hand" components availability. Depending on the complexity of the organization's materials flow, components can be delivered to a "supermarket" location close to the production process cell to be delivered to the individual production process cell locations as required by a "pull system" or Andon signal.

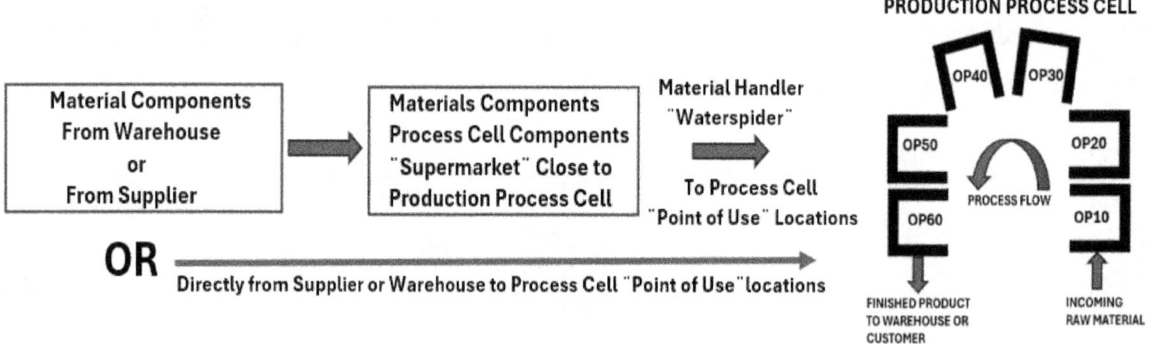

Level Loading (Heijunka).

With a balanced cell design, the organization is ready to implement level loading capacity planning and production planning. Level Loading is a capacity planning and production scheduling methodology utilizing pre-calculated average demand quantities in order to reduce operational quantity variation. The production cell can be planned and loaded according to the balanced Takt time cell design. If there are significant fluctuations in customer demand, operator available hours could be adjusted, or a redesign of the production cell balancing based on a revised Takt time calculation. For optimal results, the Level Loading scheduling methodology should be used as a sub-component of the Design for Flow Methodology.

Set-up Wheel Methodology

The Kaizen team should also work with the current state production cell operations changeover data, and the production planning team to develop the Set-up Wheel tool.

The Set-up Wheel is a Production Planning Methodology utilizing Family Product Groups, or an individual part number matrix to indicate the most efficient operational change over effort/time when (1) scheduling from one part number to another within a product group (2) scheduling from one product group to another product group. It is most efficient when used within the Design for Flow Methodology.

Physical Cell Design.

For consolidated and sequenced operations process cells, either a U shaped design or Straight design are most commonly used. An illustration of both designs is shown below.

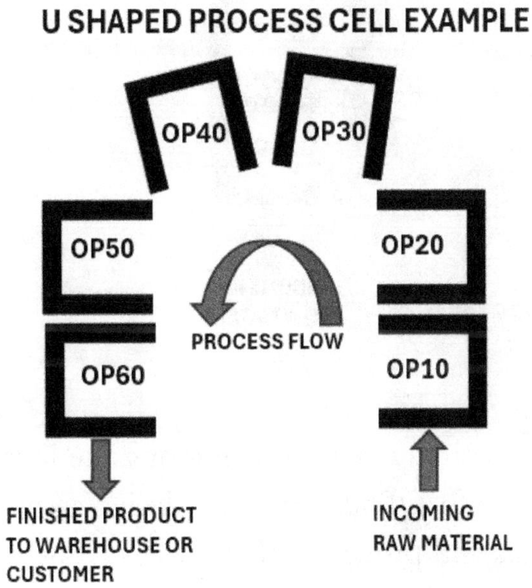

The U Shaped production cell with raw materials entering the process from OP10 and finished products exiting the cell from the OP60. This works well for facilities that have process cells located adjacent to the aisleway where both raw material components and finished products can be transported via the aisleway.

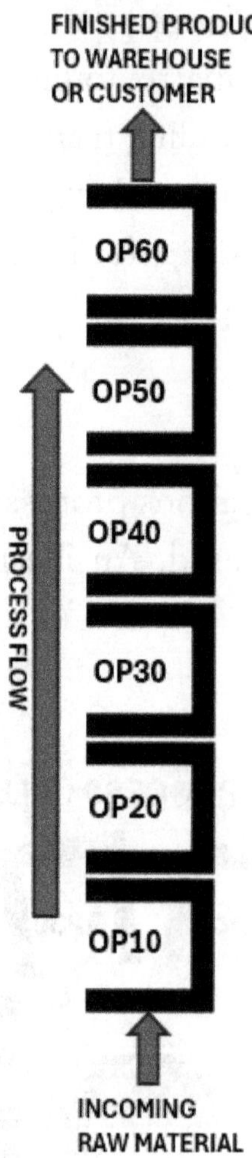

The Straight Line design with raw materials entering the line from OP10 and finished product exiting the cell from OP60. This cell design is usually a sub-design of the complete facility materials and processes flow design. Raw materials and components would enter the process from one side of the facility, move to manufacturing processing, then to assembly, and shipping to the customer. Ideally, all processing is in a straight line flow through the entire facility.

Creating Flow Methodology Overview

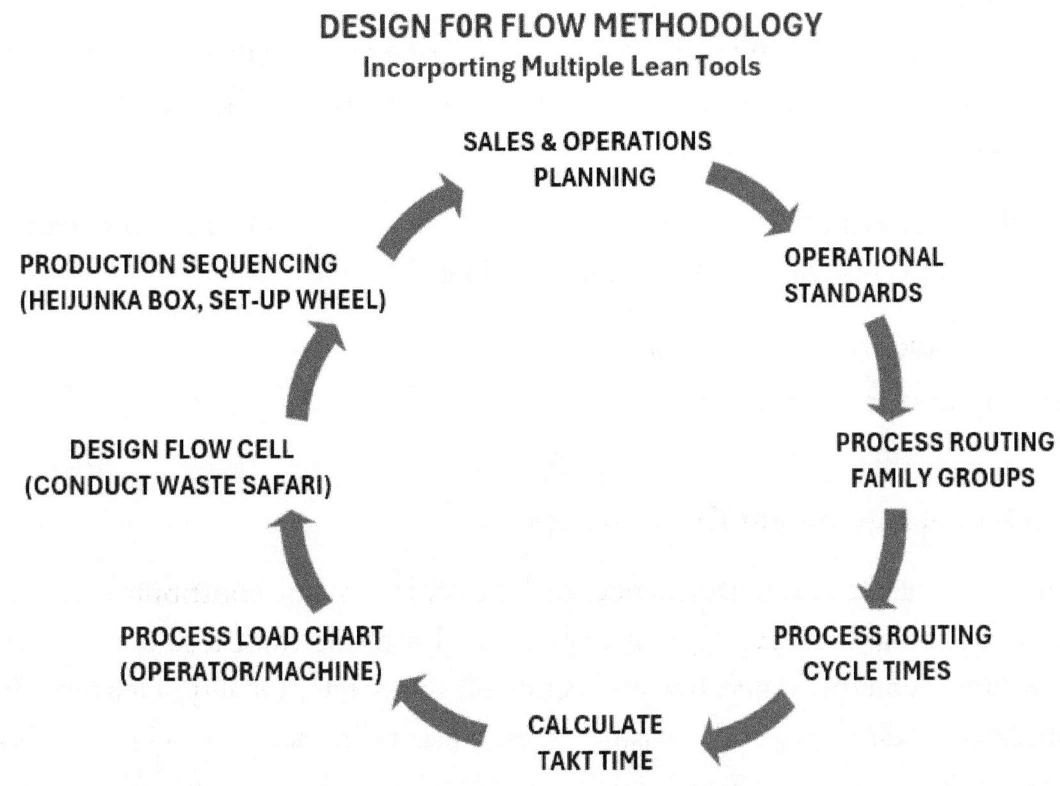

Gemba Methodology discipline regarding waste identification training, 5S/6S, equipment reliability, escalation process, operator process skill training (training matrix), and safety & quality empowerment are key contributors to Design for Flow implementation and sustainability. The above examples are focused on a manufacturing process cell balancing and design, but the basic Lean Methodology of cycle times, takt time, capacity planning, level loading, current state and future state load charting, and waste elimination can be applied to most processes.

The Design for Flow Methodology offers multiple advantages over batch scheduling or non-cellular designs.

- A more agile operational production system that is not waiting for long production runs to finish.
- More predictable planning and operational results by consolidating standard production quantities.
- Reduced lead time to the customer using just-in-time customer quantity, or product group scheduling.
- Reduced necessity for Work In Process or Finished Products inventory.
- Reduced production changeovers, especially if used with the Set-up Wheel Methodology.

Flow cells do offer multiple advantages over batch or non-cellular plant layouts. But flow cells require sustained flow culture discipline since they:

- Require dedicated equipment and/or personnel.
- Are very intolerant to waste.

OEE (Overall Equipment Effectiveness)

Equipment available and performance, or lack of, is a major contributor to waste on the manufacturing floor. Equipment unplanned downtime can cause chaos across the manufacturing enterprise negatively affecting all the Safety, Quality, Delivery, & Cost performance indicators, and causing great disappointment among stakeholders. Equipment downtime can be demoralizing to associates who are engaged in the success of the business, only to be stopped time and time again for repetitive equipment issues. This is especially true if associates compensation calculations includes productivity.

But as valuable as OEE is, it is also perhaps one of the most misunderstood or abused tool in the Lean Manufacturing Toolbox. Managers may quote OEE percentages sometimes confusing the metric with productivity or efficiency. Organizations may use the OEE percentage as an end game metric without really understanding how to use the tool, nor the power of the tool to identify and reduce or eliminate waste. OEE's value to the organization as a waste identification tool is sometimes overshadowed by a 'check the box' mentality to just post the OEE percentage on a visual management board.

This may be because the use of OEE requires real due diligence. Real time equipment monitoring and accurate identification of reason coding for downtime or performance issues are required. Equipment automatic data acquisition systems are not always in use, and when they are, accurate reason coding may still be dependent on human interface or interpretation. Performance data analysis is required in order to determine equipment performance main pains and where to concentrate Kaizen improvement efforts. If an organization is still dealing with instability at Gemba, this will make the OEE due diligence initiative even more daunting.

OEE – The Metric

The metric is comprised of three contributors as below.

- Availability %: The ratio of the planned equipment availability time vs the actual equipment availability.
- Performance %: The ratio of the planned (or optimal) production rate vs the actual production rate.
- Quality %: The ratio of the planned number of acceptable units vs the actual number of acceptable units.

Availability % X Performance % X Quality % = OEE %

OEE – The Tool

Organizations would be better off to think of the OEE metric only as an "Are We Improving" gauge. They should concentrate their efforts on the data acquisition tools and Kaizen methods required for improvement. By doing this, the organization can better focus on real improvement initiatives, and the metric gauge will improve automatically.

Below are suggestions for OEE improvement efforts.

- First the organization needs accurate Availability, Performance and Quality Data. The organization should review their data collection methodology. Is it automatic, manual, or hybrid? Is the data collection equipment adequate? Does hardware or software require upgrading? Without accurate data, it will be difficult to identify root cause issues and develop sustainable countermeasures.

- Establish an OEE reporting policy and process. It is important that the reporting methodology is uniform and consistent (standardized work) across the entire enterprise. This would include data acquisition instructions and reason codes to be used. If there are reporting gaps or deficiencies in the OEE data, this needs to be corrected immediately.

- Select "main pain" equipment to monitor. Organizations often already know where their equipment's main pains are, even if they do not have all of the root cause data. It would be better to start the program on a limited number of main pain equipment and realize real OEE gains rather than attempting a shotgun approach across all equipment.

- Dedicate the resources necessary to adequately analyze the data. Depending on organizational complexity, this can be segregated by plant, cost center, or work center. There should be a standardized methodology for data collection, data analysis, and countermeasure development, implementation, and improvement tracking.

- Use Kaizen methodology for OEE improvement projects, to include improvement sustainability tracking. This is a great method to not only implement improvements, but to involve and engage associates in the sustainable improvement actions.

- Modify or establish standards for improvement countermeasures (change management) accountability for improvement sustainability. Operators, supervisors, engineers, and managers should all have an accountability role to ensure that improvement standards are adhered to through Standardized Work, Gemba Methodology, and Daily Management.

SMED (Single Minute Exchange of Dies).

SMED is another of the Lean Tools in the "Pursuit of Perfection" Lean Toolbox. The Methodology can be used to reduce waste in any situation where a process is waiting for a changeover of operational resources, normally equipment or materials. But the methodology can also be used for back office indirect processes as well. SMED Is a perfect example of a situation where an engineer may concentrate to improve equipment cycle time (VA) while ignoring the "waste" of excessive equipment changeover time (NVA).

An overview of the SMED recipe is shown below.

- Select the area to perform the SMED event. This is better achieved through performance data acquisition either electronically or manually, as discussed above in the OEE section. Depending on the complexity of the changeover activities, a Kaizen team should be used for efficiency, employee training and to foster associate engagement.

- Measure the time of each of the changeover activities, from stop of previous process (last production part) to the start of the new process (1st production piece). Measure individual activities and video the changeover process for additional review by the Kaizen team.

- Categorize the individual change over activities by:
  - <u>Internal Activities</u>: These are change over activities that occur after the stop of the previous process (last part off).
  - <u>External Activities</u>: These are changeover activities that occur prior to the stopping of the previous process. These activities should not interfere with the production of the previous process but occur as the previous process is running.

- Review the current state categorized activities to determine:
  - If internal categorized activities can be moved to external activities in order to reduce the time that the new process equipment is actually stopped pending completion of change over activities. For example, a molding operation stops the previous operation before retrieving the molding tooling for the next operation set up. This activity could be reorganized so that the molding tooling is retrieved while the previous operation is running. In this manner the tooling will be ready for changeover when the previous operation stops.
  - Are there activities that can be improved by equipment or process modifications? For example, adding quick change hose connection fittings instead of existing manual change fittings.

- Conduct the Waste Safari during the measuring of both internal and external individual change over activities, and during a review of the video of activities. Are there activities that are not necessary and can be eliminated? Are there necessary activities that can be reduced without negatively affecting the integrity of changeover activities? Refer to the Gemba Culture eight wastes.
- Conduct a "Safety Safari". Are there activities that are considered as risk to associates? This can also be accomplished during the Waste Safari described above. Lockout/Tagout procedures should be reviewed and training performed for all SMED event involved personnel. Changes to operational standards should be reviewed and approved by the appropriate organization Safety resource prior to implementation.

- Once the above activities are completed, make a draft change to the current changeover Operational Standards, and train the appropriate personnel (engineers, operators, HSE personnel, etc.)

- Execute the actual draft changeover process. Make any additional modifications and/or improvements. Complete the revised Change Over Operational Standard (change management).

- Follow the organization's Kaizen project close and Site Improvement Planning guidelines.

TPM (Total Productive Maintenance)

TPM is another of the "Pursuit of Perfection" Lean Tool Box tools. Equipment performance can be a major factor in the ability of the organization to meet Safety, Quality, Delivery, & Cost objectives. Equipment that is not adequately maintained can cause issues such as Safety Hazards, Downtime, Poor Efficiency, Quality Defects, and negatively affect employee morale. As discussed in the Design for Flow section, flow production cells do not tolerate waste such as equipment downtime.

The TPM Methodology's purpose is to eliminate safety risks and downtime, and to improve equipment related quality and efficiency. TPM is an enterprise wide methodology that covers the spectrum from basic equipment performance to new equipment design and funding. For the purpose of the Kaizen Tools and Culture unit, the aspects of performing an TPM Kaizen Improvement Event are addressed.

- Select the equipment to be included in the Kaizen Improvement event. This is better achieved through performance data acquisition either electronically or manually, as discussed above in the OEE section. Also utilizing the Safety, Quality, Delivery, & Cost priority filter may help in the selection process. Equipment that presents risks to Safety or Quality should be immediately stopped and appropriate countermeasures applied. As part of a TPM policy and process, employees should be empowered to stop equipment or processes that present a Safety or Quality risk.

- Understand the selected equipment current state performance data. This is better achieved through performance data acquisition either electronically or manually, and historic maintenance records data. Also, operator input may be valuable during this part of the process and is a good method to verify maintenance issues, and to solicit associate engagement in the improvement process.

- Perform an Equipment "Safety Safari". Review for upgrades to equipment safety features (guarding, Estops, sensors, etc). Lockout/Tagout procedures should be reviewed and training performed for all TPM personnel involved. All changes to operational standards should be reviewed and approved by the appropriate organization Safety resource prior to implementation.

- Develop the equipment future state improvements list. Ideally use a Kaizen Team of equipment integrity stakeholders and other subject matter experts to develop the future state equipment improvement plan. Review the improvements lists for funding requirements. The organization's Finance Capital Equipment Funding process may be required for major repair costs or equipment replacement funding.

- Implement the future state improvements list. Develop performance metrics and data acquisition for future state performance tracking. Also, it is necessary to coordinate any equipment downtime due to TPM modifications with the organization's production planning.

- Develop and implement future state maintenance and training programs:

- Preventative Maintenance: An improved time or usage maintenance program to provide adequate maintenance to the equipment based on the current state maintenance data information, and any additional future state maintenance requirements.
- Autonomous Maintenance: A maintenance program provided by equipment operators for basic equipment maintenance such as performance monitoring, cleaning, lubrication, and inspection. Autonomous maintenance promotes employee engagement among both operators and maintenance personnel. The Autonomous Maintenance Program should be reviewed by the organization's maintenance and safety resources to assure that no risks to operator personnel exist. Also, Autonomous Maintenance Program formats should be included in the Gemba Visual Management processes.

- Make necessary Standardized Work documentation (change management) for changes to operational standards, preventative, and autonomous maintenance programs.

VA/VE (Value Analysis/Value Engineering)

VA/VE is a set of innovative Lean waste reduction tools that are not as heavily advertised as some of the above reviewed Lean tools, but targeted to the right applications, their results can be impressive. The Value Analysis tool is used primarily for existing products, while Value Engineering is used primarily for new products design. For the purpose of this Kaizen Tools and Culture unit, the focus will be on the use of the Value Analysis tool.

The primary purpose of the Value Analysis tool is to review existing products for possible waste and cost reduction while still adhering to customer's use and quality specifications. Value Analysis is best performed as a Kaizen Event involving product and process stakeholders and other subject matter experts as required. Steps to perform a Value Analysis Kaizen are shown below.

- Select the product(s) for the Kaizen Event. A Value Analysis Kaizen may be the necessity of marketplace competitiveness, or organizational strategy to increase sales profit margin.

- Select Kaizen Event participants. Since a Value Analysis exercise should review processing, materials, and product specifications, stakeholders from all disciplines should be selected.

- Collect the data regarding:
  - Processing steps, equipment, times. Similar to a Design for Flow event.
  - Raw materials and purchased components cost, suppliers and materials composition.
  - Product specifications, customer requirements, and competitor's products specifications. Product information can also be collected via customer surveys and focus groups, as necessary.

- The Kaizen team should analyze data points for product, process, and materials attributes, comparing current state attributes to an ideal future state configuration.

- The Kaizen team will develop the proposed list of attributes waste/cost reduction. This list may have multiple team reviews in order to select the most feasible final proposal. The final proposal should include any implementation cost, capital investment, and materials obsolescence data.

- A financial cost reduction verification analysis should be performed before implementation of waste/cost reduction initiatives. The financial verification should also include any implementation cost, capital investment, and materials obsolescence, as necessary.

- Presentation of a final cost of current state vs future state processing and product attribute changes proposal to the appropriate organization management stakeholders. These may include commercial materials, operations, finance and engineering.

- Depending on the complexity of proposed changes, beta testing or focus group testing may be required prior to full proposal implementation.

- A future state product phase in implementation date should be determined. Customer notifications, if required, should be considered. Use up or elimination cost of obsolete inventory should also be considered when phasing out current state processes and products. Materials obsolescence is a direct debit to the Profit & Loss.

- Final processing and product attribute changes to be incorporated into the organization's change management process.

Material Pull Systems

Inventory replenishment systems normally use two methodologies, Push and Pull replenishment. Organizations decide to use either, or hybrids, based on their business inputs. If a business model has very stable demand and forecasting, they may decide to use a Push system. Many Materials Requirements Planning (MRP) systems manage both Push and Pull systems.

Push systems normally drive replenishment signals from top level (finished or subassembly products) forecasting, although forecasts can be created at almost any level of the products Bill of Materials (BOM). As a simple explanation, forecasts are uploaded into the organization's MRP system. The MRP system performs calculations based on stock on hand + forecasted receipts – forecasted usage and creates signals to produce or purchase more inventory. There are other influences based on how the organization's MRP set-up data (or master data) is configured, but these are not included in the above calculation just to keep the explanation simple.

This works OK in a perfect world, but forecasting, while a science, is almost never an accurate science, thus inventory creation signals may come too early or too late. Also, there is the exponential damage to customer delivery and cost caused by pushing MRP forecast data through all the internal and external influences caused by variables in the manufacturing processes and global supply chain.

An example of various types of manufacturing and supply chain variables affecting an MRP Push system are shown below.

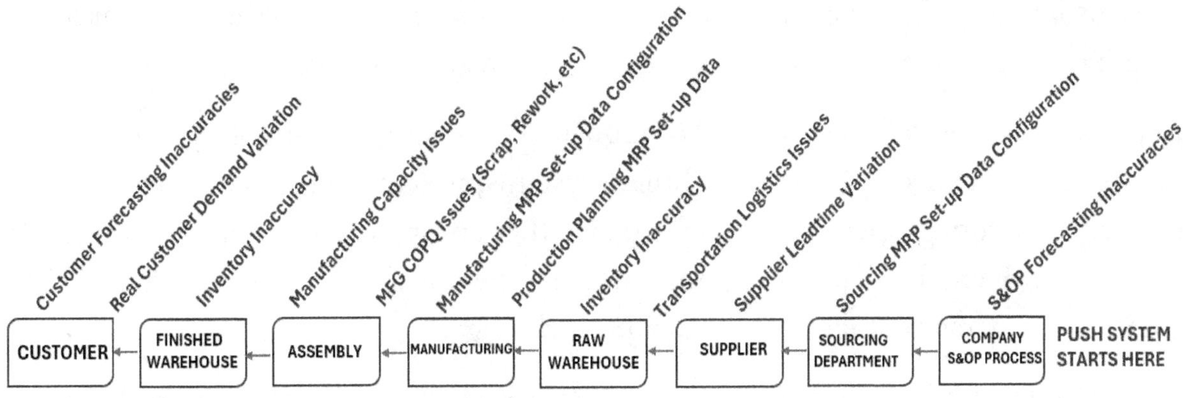

PUSH SYSTEMS INTEGRITY DAMAGE CAUSED BY PUSHING DEMAND THROUGH FORECASTING, MANUFACTURING & SUPPLY CHAIN VARIABLES

On the other hand, a correctly designed Pull system ideally starts with real customer demand, not forecasted customer demand. When items are allocated to customers, a precalculated replenishment signal is generated to backfill the allocated inventory. This type of Pull system can be configured to generate replenishment signals through all manufacturing processes, and to the raw materials/components suppliers.

A correctly designed Pull system can have real wastes/costs elimination opportunities to include:

- Reduction of Finished and Work in Process Inventory since the replenishment signals are created by real demand and not forecasted Push demand.

- A Kanban type Pull system can drastically improve deliveries to customers by providing just in time customer delivery.

- Improved manufacturing efficiency since associates and equipment are only focused on real demand and not on producing excessive forecasted demand, or expediting under forecasted demand.

- Improved associate engagement and morale since non-value efforts have been reduced or eliminated.

But Pull systems do not come without effort. They require a high level of due diligence whether using kanban cards, containers, virtual signals, or any other type of pull signals. Lack of control of pull signals can be devastating to the Pull system's integrity. Pull systems integrity should be included in the organization´s Visual Management System, Gemba Methodology, and Management Gemba Walking wherever possible.

Also, Pull systems do not completely eliminate the forecasting variable. Forecasting may still be required for supplier replenishment systems, systems capacity planning, and non-pull manufacturing operations. The broader that an organization can implement Pull systems in their manufacturing and materials operations, the less they fall victim to forecast inaccuracy compounded MRP push damage.

An example of a Pull System with the replenishment signal started by real customer demand.

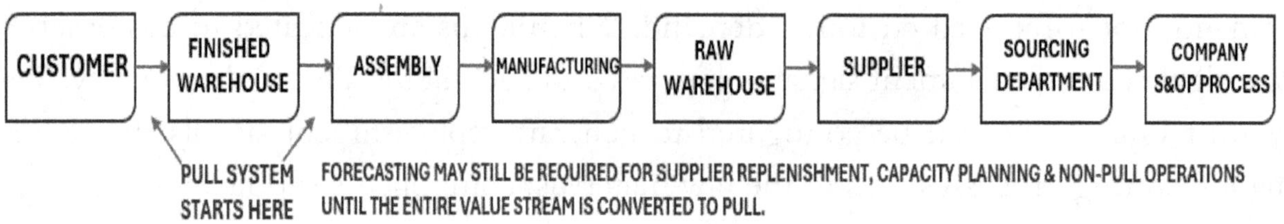

Referring again to the Lean Journey Roadmap below, establishing pull is recommended after implementation of Gemba stability and Kaizen waste elimination Tools.

There are good reasons for this sequencing order of Tools and Cultures.

- Both Push and Pull systems will be interrupted by instability at Gemba.

- The organization must understand well their Value Stream and eliminate Value Stream wastes.

- Pull systems require the sustainable discipline provided by Lean tools such as 5S, waste elimination (inventory is waste), Just in Time Flow manufacturing reduced lead times, and rapid changeover for smaller lots production.

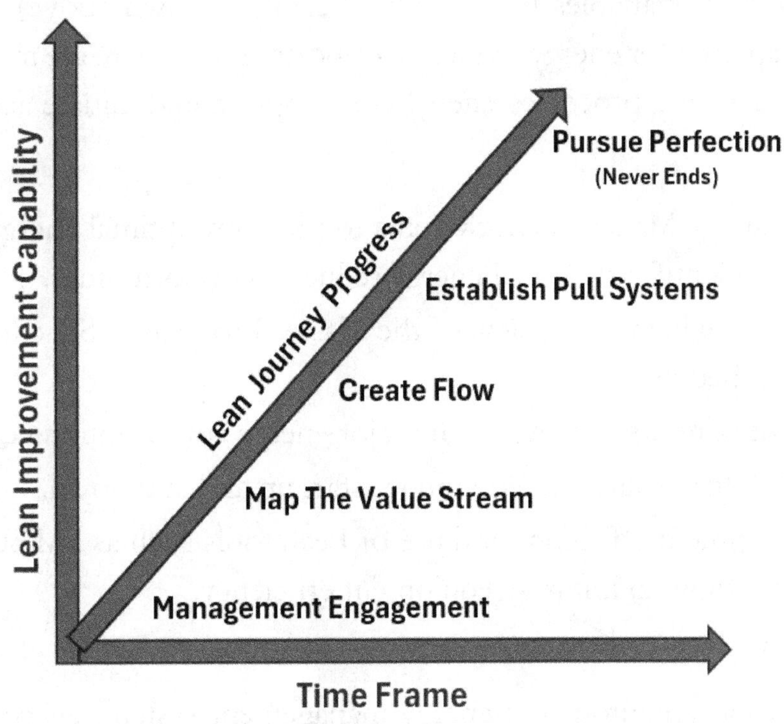

Energy Usage and Carbon Footprint Reduction

The cost of energy consumption in manufacturing processes can be a major cost factor. Some studies indicate that up to 10% of production cost can be for electricity alone. Of course, the cost of facility energy depends on several factors.

- Type of manufacturing
- Location
- Equipment efficiency
- Facility age
- Operating hours
- Energy cost offset initiatives (solar panels, etc)

Energy waste reduction is sometimes thought of as a fixed expense, or a hard to deal with variable expense, and for those reasons is sometimes overlooked as a Profit & Loss savings contributor.

Just as there are input variables to the cost of energy (shown above), these variables should also be explored for energy reduction opportunities. There are methods available to investigate facility and processes energy consumption and initiate actions to reduce consumption and cost.

- Automated Energy Management Systems to program optimal energy consumption schedules, and identify additional energy reduction opportunities.
- Facility shifts scheduling. A review of the Master Production Schedule aligned with optimal shift scheduling.
- Energy cost peak hours scheduling of major energy consumption equipment.
- Standard Work for facility and equipment start up and shutdown.
- Review of equipment efficiency and use of Lean tools such as SMED, OEE, TPM, and Design for Flow to improve equipment efficiency.
- Perform a Lean Energy Kaizen.

Even if a facility has an automated energy management system, energy consumption waste may still exist. Depending on the size and complexity of a facility and processes, an Energy Kaizen has the potential for significant results. The process is outlined below:

- Develop a Kaizen team comprised of resources familiar with the facility's energy consumption sources. These team members may be from maintenance, engineering, supervisors, etc. Also, an external subject matter expert can be included in the tea.
- Develop an energy walk schedule to physically walk the facility and all processes during all shifts, including all non-working shifts. All support areas (compressors, chillers, pumps, etc) and indirect areas (offices and plant support areas) are to be included in the schedule.
- Develop a list of energy consumption sources that are not required during particular shifts. It is important to not overlook equipment that should be operating, but is operating inefficiently (compressed air leaks, inefficient lighting sources).
- Develop a list of energy consumption actions, and verify with the facility management team. Upon verification of the action list, assign an energy savings calculation to each of the action items. The savings calculation should also be calculated in monetary savings.
- Develop an actions implementation schedule. A four quad cost/benefit analysis can be used to identify the best sequence of actions implementation. Identified savings actions that cannot be programmed into an Energy Management System should be

incorporated into departmental Standard Work, such as facility/equipment start-up and shut down procedures.

- Develop an energy consumption tracker to ensure that projected savings are being realized. The tracker should include actions, implementation scheduling, responsible personnel for implementation, and an anticipated savings calendar. This tracker will also be an input to Site Improvement Planning tool.

Materials Management & Sourcing Savings

Material Management has a vast span of responsibilities as it relates to operations performance and the overall Lean Business System. Depending on the complexity of the business, below are some disciplines that span the Materials Management area of responsibility:

- Customer Demand Planning
- Demand Forecasting Management
- Materials Requirements Planning Management
- Inventory Storage, Security, and Accuracy
- Work in Process Inventory Management
- Maintenance, Repair, and Operating supplies management.
- Materials Logistics (raw materials in & finished goods out)
- Supplier Management (Quality, Lead Times, Payment Terms, Production Schedules)
- Customs Regulations (Import & Export)

With such a wide span of control, Materials Management is a major contributor to the Lean Business System, either favorably or not so favorably. Examples of their contribution to the Kaizen Tools & Culture methodology, as well as the other four Lean Business System building blocks are shown below.

- **Management Methodology:**

  - Participate as a high level echelon manager in the organization's management team.

- Ensure that all Materials Management team members are Lean Methodology and Materials Management skills trained (training matrix).
- Be highly engaged in all five Lean Business System building blocks.

- **Gemba Methodology:**
  - Configuration of Enterprise Resource Planning and Materials Requirements Planning data to deliver raw materials & components as required by the Master Production Schedule.
  - Collaborate with Operations to ensure that Maintenance, Repair, & Operating (MRO) materials planning provide materials and services as required.
  - Provide supplier continuous improvement quality.
  - Participation in Visual Management Gemba tier level meetings.
  - Ensure security and integrity of raw materials, components, and MRO materials inventories.
  - Ensure that all Materials Management team members are adequately engaged in the production Gemba processes as required.

- **Kaizen Methodology:**
  - Maintain a Materials Management Site Improvement Planning tool. This tool will list and track all Materials Management & Sourcing specific savings, and will be an Input into the organization's main Site Improvement Planning tool.
  - Consistent negotiation of Best Value (lowest cost, best quality, best delivery) of:
    *Production raw materials & components.
    *MRO materials & related services.
    *Fixed overhead supplier contracts.
    *Logistics and related services contracts (including customs).

- **Finance Methodology:**
  - Ensure compliance to Materials Management responsible Profit & Loss accounts, and budgeting performance metrics.
  - Provide best possible materials and services forward budgeting information accuracy.
  - Collaborate with all department managers to identify and implement waste reduction and cost savings across all of the organization's business disciplines.

- Optimal planning of Inventory carrying cost, storage, and accuracy as it relates to the organization's working capital.
-Suppliers inventory/delivery and payment terms cash flow management. Also considering supplier stocking, JIT delivery, consignment type programs.

- **Strategy Methodology:**
  - Participate as a high echelon level manager in the organization's Strategy Planning, Deployment, and Achievement Process.
  - Ensure that Materials Management strategy planning objectives are cascading deployed and achieved.

Kaizen Events - Kaizen Events Calendar

Since many of the Lean improvement tools discussed in this unit utilize Kaizen Teams and Kaizen Events, now is a good time to review the basic framework of the Kaizen Event.

The Kaizen event is an organized methodology to employ dedicated personnel resources (usually multi-disciplinary) to develop and implement improvements to a particular Safety, Quality, Delivery, & Cost opportunity, or any other main pain opportunity. Kaizen events ideally should be an output of the Site Improvement Planning process, meaning that the waste/cost reduction opportunity has been feasibility verified, prioritized, and approved by the Site Improvement Steering Committee.

Kaizen events should be scheduled in advance, ideally for a fixed rolling timeframe calendar. The Kaizen Calendar should list the name of the event, the dates of the event, and ideally all the selected participants for the event. This allows participants and their managers to be optimally prepared to support the event, as well as their own departmental tasks. Kaizen event participation is a foundation initiative for the development of Highly Engaged-High Performance Lean Teams. Refer to the circular Lean training methodology discussed in the Management Tools & Culture Unit.

Kaizen events usually have a common set of guidelines:

•A Kaizen Event Charter. The Charter is the official document that the event is authorized by the steering committee to proceed. The Charter should include as a minimum:

- The event title

- The event scope and description (problem statement)

-The Lean Methodology or Six Sigma tool(s) to be employed during the event

- The event objective, current state performance metrics and targeted future state performance metrics. Ideally, the performance targets should include the Financial Profit & Loss accounts to be improved.

- The event schedule and participants.

•It is important to have multi-disciplinary team members that have knowledge of the problem statement. The team selection should also include the event sponsor, event leader, process owner, and subject matter expert(s) if required.

•The Kaizen Event is ideally a rapid improvement process and should be scheduled within a firm time schedule, normally within a working week, or sooner. The event sponsor and leader should decide if prework is required in order to comply with the firm schedule. Examples of prework might include data gathering, processes investigation, materials availability, etc.

•Event participants should be trained regarding the Event Charter and the particular Lean or Six Sigma Methodology to be used in the event. This can be accomplished as prework or during the event. Reference the "Associate Training & Engagement" section covered in Management Tools & Culture Unit.

•During the event, a daily event report should be scheduled to review:

- Tasks actually accomplished vs tasks planned for the current day, and a description of tasks planned for the following work day.

- Overall event schedule compliance. Is the event on schedule, or is scheduling countermeasure required?

- Obstacles that need to be resolved for event success.

- Resources needed from the event sponsor or management team.

•The event should be concluded with the approval of the event sponsor. A formal event conclusion report should be generated. This conclusion report out should display actual results compared to the event Charter planned results. This should show all improvements made during the event and improvements scheduled to be completed after the event conclusion (event newspaper).

•Ideally the event leader and participants should prepare a conclusion presentation to be formally presented to management and other interested stakeholders. (sister plants, division personnel, etc.). The presentation event is an important contribution to employee engagement as all event participants have an opportunity to present. The presentation should also be made available to the entire employee population.

•The organization should sponsor a team celebration for the work completed during the event. Celebrating success is motivation for participants to be continuous improvement engaged and involved in future events. The presentation and celebration are also motivation to recruit and engage future event participants.

The event conclusion report information is an input to the Site Improvement Sustainability Tracker, measuring actual results vs planned results.

Pursuit Of Perfection Mindset.

Lean practitioners are quick to remind us that "it's not about the tools; it's about involving the people". This is almost true. To build the Lean Business System Culture, it requires excellence in both mastering the tools and mastering associate engagement. One without the other will not yield the "Pursuit of Perfection" mindset and culture that the Lean Business System Methodology requires.

Management must be continually engaged in the "Pursuit of Perfection" methodology by mentoring and allowing associates to fail and succeed. Understanding and promoting the philosophies that "Delayed Perfection" is immensely counterproductive, and that "Dropping an Egg" along the path of Continuous Improvement is not fatal.

Profit & Loss accountable personnel and Continuous Improvement personnel should be consistently performing wastes/costs main pain analysis. An analysis tool such as an 80/20 pareto is simple to understand by all personnel and can be used to visibly highlight wastes/costs reduction/elimination opportunities.

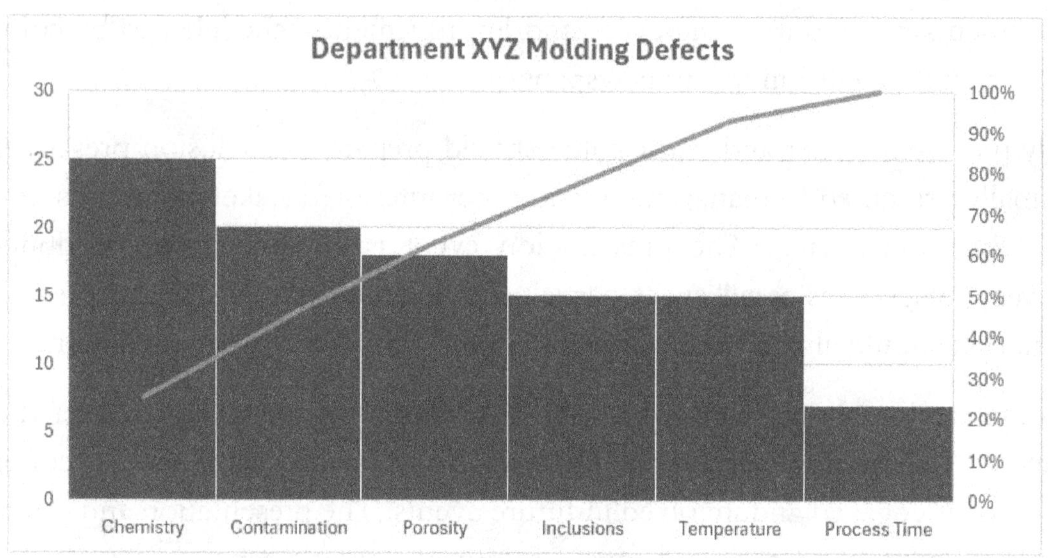

For example, the above Pareto analysis highlights the Main Pains for the XYZ department molding defects. Accountable personnel close to this Gemba area should see this type of daily waste, but simple analysis may display a clearer picture of which issue(s) they should attack first or in parallel. This may also present additional opportunities for waste and costs reduction as inputs to the organization's Site Improvement Planning.

Waste hunting by managers, cost accountants, and Lean practitioners should be a consistent and continuous effort in the Lean Business System "Pursuit of Perfection" culture.

Burn the Boats - Enjoy the Journey

UNIT 4 – FINANCIAL TOOLS & CULTURE

Financial Alignment and Accountability

The Profit & Loss (Income Statement)

A profit and loss statement (P&L) is a financial report that provides a summary of a company's revenues, expenses, and profits/losses over a given period of time. The Profit & Loss statement shows a company's ability to generate sales, manage expenses, and create profits, all of which are of great importance to all stakeholders.

Quite simply put:

REVENUES — EXPENSES = A PROFIT OR A LOSS

The health of the organization's Profit & Loss is vitally important to all involved Stakeholders. If the Profit & Loss statement is not healthy, it is possible that the company cannot pay its employees, cannot buy inventory to convert into products to sale to customers, cannot satisfy shareholders who are expecting a return on their investment, and can also affect local businesses who are depending on employees to buy their goods and services.

It was discussed in the "Gemba Tools & Culture" how Safety, Quality, Delivery, & Cost stabilization at the Gemba level can favorably affect the organization's Profit & Loss. The Kaizen Tools and Culture business improvements stacked upon the Gemba Tools & Culture stability offers almost infinite Profit & Loss improvement opportunities, as shown below. And this is only a partial listing of Profit & Loss expenses that offer improvement opportunities.

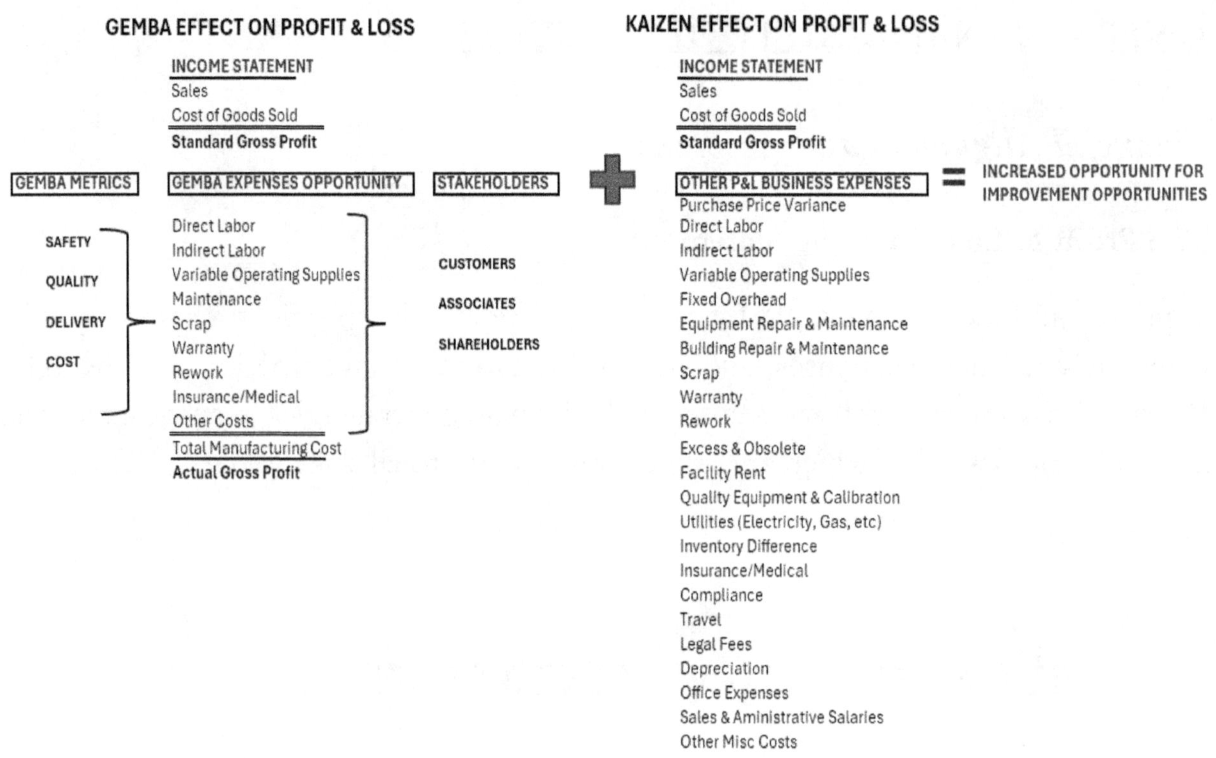

Lean Manufacturing or Lean Business Systems Transformation at times receives negative reviews by top echelon management because they cannot visibly link the transformation efforts to actual Profit & Loss results. Lean practitioners and operations managers do not always speak the same "Financeze" language as do top echelon management. Financial managers should be responsible for ensuring that Lean practitioners and department Profit & Loss responsible managers understand the Profit & Loss format, and that they understand the revenue or expense detail of their particular departments.

A finance executive should not allow anyone in the organization to submit Profit & Loss budget information that is deemed suspect or not achievable. Financial "Stretch Goals" are financially healthy for the organization if substantiated by potentially viable revenue or savings opportunities.

Increasing Costs, Pricing & Profit

In a financial incremental budgeting process, the organization may start with the previous year expenses (or current year to date) data to calculate a baseline for the following year profit & loss expense data, and then apply increases or decreases to this data based on change expectations data.

The Lean Business System is designed to continually reduce waste and unnecessary costs. The System is designed to reduce current year costs and forecastable future costs. Without this continuous improvement, most businesses can use a straight line method to project increased cost and reduced margins, and when they will eventually have to close their doors. It is impractical to think that all year-over-year inflationary cost increases can simply be passed to customers with no effect on profit. It is also impractical to think that competitors are not aware of the Lean Business System methodology. And to stress margins even more, many customers include future pricing reductions in their sourcing agreements.

The inability to achieve relentless and sustainable wastes/costs reduction will have a direct impact on business operating profitability. The fact is that most business expenses will increase year-over-year. Robust countermeasures are required in order to maintain a healthy Profit & Loss. These countermeasures are in the form of relentless Gemba & Kaizen waste reduction; negotiation of materials cost, variable costs, and costs normally considered as fixed costs; and correct sales pricing/margin evaluation.

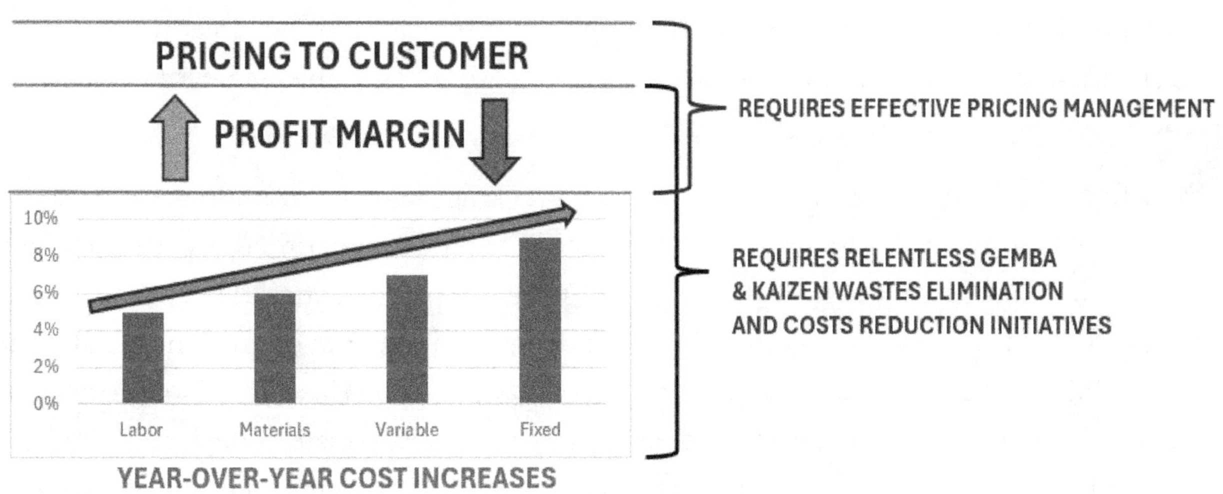

Poor Pricing Management is not normally considered as a Lean Manufacturing waste, but it is a Lean Business System potential waste to be considered. Cost is certainly a major contributor to customer pricing, but there are other important inputs to consider. The business must understand the marketplace and competitor's pricing strategy, product technical and quality comparisons, and the ability to deliver per customer request. Also pricing agreements and contracts must be reviewed prior to expiration in order to assure pricing accuracy. In the Lean Business System, pricing can be referred to as a potential 9th waste.

While the examples above may appear simplistic, they should not be taken lightly. According to the U.S. Bureau of Labor Statistics, the 10-year survival rate for the manufacturing industry is 43.6%. While failure rates can vary by industry, location, and economic conditions, it should be safe to assume that a manufacturing business with a robust Lean Business System will have a much better chance of survival than those that don't embrace the methodology. The Lean Business System is designed to reduce waste and cost and deliver profit improvement through "Strategic" continuous improvement initiatives.

Key Financial Performance Indicators - Root Cause & Countermeasure

Every key financial Profit & Loss account should have a responsible and accountable account owner. Financial management should ensure that department managers understand which accounts they are responsible for. These department managers should be involved in the financial budgeting process and be able to track the performance of their responsible accounts through a daily management process or check book type monitoring process.

Key financial Profit & Loss accounts that are tracking negative to budget expectations must have a Root Cause & Countermeasure analysis performed by the account responsible in order to correct the projected negative performance. This process must be performed as real time as possible. A management review of month-to-date and projected month close Income Statement status, with Root Cause & Countermeasure (if applicable) should be performed at least weekly. Adequately designed financial accounts leading indicator daily management can aid immensely in preventing weekly/monthly financial variances surprises. Waiting until the month end Income Statement financial close process is not an effective Root Cause/Countermeasure process.

Site Improvement Planning Process

Now that management and associates are better trained and increasingly engaged to improve Gemba stability (Gemba Tools & Culture) and to make real sustainable Kaizen improvements (Kaizen Tools & Culture) across all business Profit & Loss opportunities, there is a need to organize and select improvement activities to ensure prioritization of resources and optimal return on efforts. A risk that can befall a highly engaged-high performance organization is the tendency to attempt to do everything at once, while in the end accomplishing very little. This type of project overloading with minimal results will frustrate and demoralize associates.

As a Continuous Improvement Tool, the Site Improvement Planning is designed to provide an organized process to:

- Capture potential business improvement projects from across the entire business enterprise.
- Review project feasibility.
- Perform a cost benefit analysis.
- Approve and prioritize higher return or main pain projects.
- Allocate resources for approved projects.
- Launch and track projects sustainability to ensure planned savings achievement.

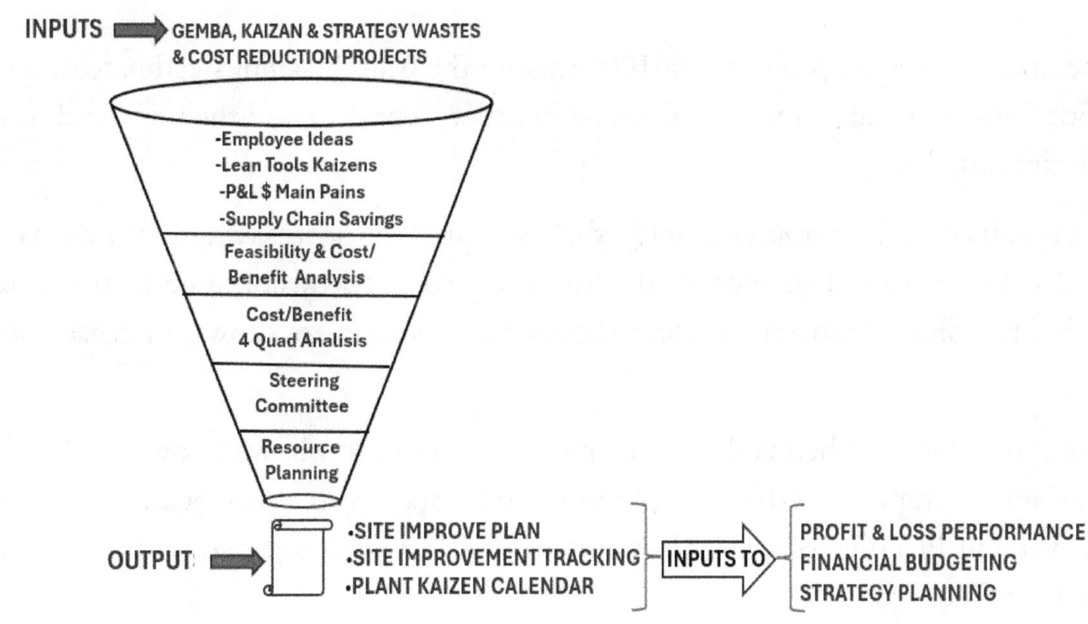

Historical revenue and expense data will not suffice for accurate budgeting, budgeting achievement, and optimal business management. The Site Improvement Planning process promotes relentless and sustainable waste elimination and cost reduction, which are major inputs to the Lean Business System Financial Tools & Culture.

Site Improvement Planning Tool

The Site Improvement Planning Tool may have different formats, but it must be agile enough to present the status of projects at every stage in order to provide all stakeholders with accurate information. An abbreviated overview example of an Excel Site Improvement Planning Tool is shown below.

Example of Site Improvement Plan Format With Monthly Results Tracking

Project Number	Project Description	Date Submitted	Project Type	Finance Account	Annual Savings	Monthly Savings	Status	C/B Score	Status Date	Leader		Jan	Feb	Mar	YTD TOTAL
S0001001	001 Assy Cell Productivity	11/15/2024	Kaizen Event	Labor Savings	$10,000	$833	Launched	2	12/10/2024	J. Smith	PLAN	$833	$833	$833	$2,499
											ACTUAL	$850	$850	$650	$2,350
S0001002	Sourcing Supplier Change	12/10/2024	Sourcing	Purchased Mtl	$50,000	$4,166	Launched	4	1/5/2025	J. Doe	PLAN	$0	4,100	$4,166	$8,266
											ACTUAL	$0	$4,150	$4,700	$8,850
S0001003	Molding Variation	1/10/2025	DMAIC	Scrap Dept xyz	$20,000	$1,666	Scheduled	4	3/1/2025	H. Lopez	PLAN				
											ACTUAL				
S0001004	Sourcing Consignment	2/1/2025	Sourcing	Inventory			Submitted	4							
S0001005	Machine Process #xxxx	1/15/2025	Kaizen Event	Labor Savings			Not Feasible								

Input to Kaizen Calendar

Use Account Names or P&L Account Numbers

Reference Status Codes on Site Improvement Plan Process

Cost/Benefit Score Based on Financial Guidlines

Project S0001001 Missed March Savings Target, Gap Countermeasured to April

In the above example, project S0001001 missed the March savings estimate, requiring a Root Cause & Countermeasure exercise in order to understand the miss, and recover for future months.

Project S0001002 is complying with the estimated project savings. March savings exceeded the projected savings. If this trend is projected to continue through future months, the Site Improvement Plan should be modified to shown increased future savings.

Project S0001003 is scheduled to start during a future month not shown in the above abbreviated example. S0001004 is submitted to be approved and scheduled by the Site Improvement Planning Steering Committee. S0001005 was rejected, but is still on the format for future reference.

The Site Improvement Planning Tool, while informative to Stakeholders, should not be thought of as only an information tool, nor as only inputs to the financial Profit & Loss achievement and budgeting process. As important as all of these aspects are, the tool is a Lean Business System cultural catalyst for the "Relentless Pursuit of Business Perfection". It should be a driving force for improvements around Safety, Quality, Delivery, Cost, Cash, and Employee Engagement.

The overall process must have a responsible owner providing constant oversight. Each project must have an assigned responsible project owner, and the process must have constant and frequent management review. An overview example of the process is shown below. The process and process flow will change with the unique requirements of each organization.

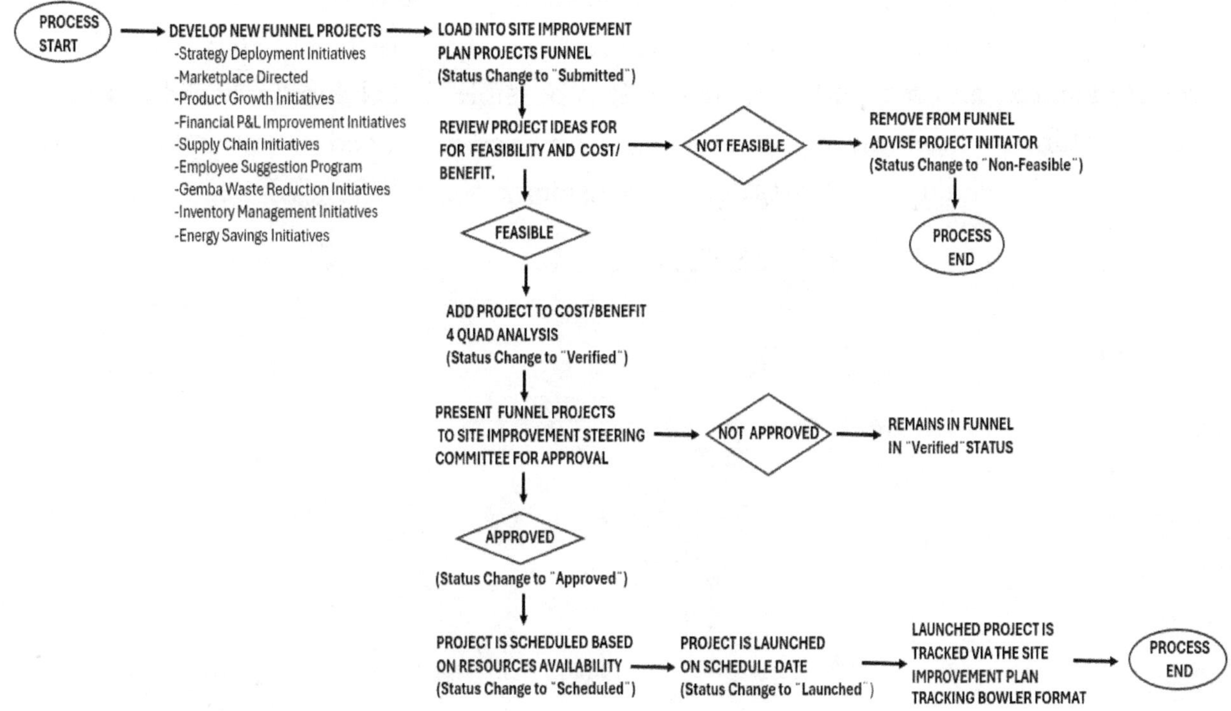

Projects Feasibility & Cost/Benefit Review

The Site Improvement Planning does not come without effort. As shown on the Funnel Diagram and Process Flow, a waste reduction suggestion entering the funnel must undergo some form of Technical Feasibility and Cost/Benefit review before reaching an approved status. The goal of the Feasibility and Cost/Benefit review is to understand the cost of the current state, the cost of implementing a solution, and the monetary benefit expected from the future state versus the current state. Most organizations have restrictions regarding Return on Investment for expense and capital expenditures funding, so funding restrictions should be considered in the initial Feasibility and Cost/Benefit review.

All proposed projects should be evaluated by appropriate technical and financial resources. To make this task a bit easier, personnel suggesting a waste/cost reduction project should complete as much of the feasibility review as possible since they are usually the most knowledgeable regarding the current state process to be improved, and the suggested future state improvement.

Suggested projects rejected for lack of feasibility should be recorded on the Site Improvement Planning format for reference, and the project initiator advised of the rejected status, and reason for rejection. It is possible that the initiator did not include sufficient information on the original suggestion and may need to revise the suggestion for further Feasibility and Cost/Benefit consideration.

An overview example of an Excel Feasibility Review Format is below.

DATE:		INITATIOR:		
CURRENT STATE WASTE STATEMENT:				
PROPOSED FUTURE STATE;				
	YEAR 1	YEAR 2	YEAR 3	
CURRENT STATE COST:				
MATERIALS:				
LABOR:				
VARIABLE EXPENSE:				
OVERHEADS:				
TOTAL COSTS:				
FUTURE STATE COST:				
MATERIALS:				
LABOR:				
VARIABLE EXPENSE:				
OVERHEADS:				
TOTAL COSTS:				
PROJECTED SAVINGS/COSTS:				
MATERIALS:				
LABOR:				
VARIABLE EXPENSE:				
OVERHEADS:				
TOTAL SAVINGS/COSTS:				
ADDITIONAL REQUIRED INVESTMENT:				
EXPENSE AMOUNT:				
CAPITAL AMOUNT:				
RETURN ON INVESTMENT MONTHS:				
FINANCIAL FEASIBILITY:	PASS:____________		FAIL:____________	
TECHNICAL FEASIBILITY REVIEW:	PASS:____________		FAIL:____________	
COST/BENEFIT SCORE:	1 HC/LB	2 LC/LB	3 HC/HB	4 LC/HB
COMMENTS:				
TECHNICAL APPROVAL:				
FINANCE APPROVAL:				

The above format example extends to three years since that is the example maximum time for the Return on Investment. The above format is only an example and would be modified to comply with an organization's financial approval guidelines.

Cost/Benefit Four Quad Classification

Improvement suggestions that are feasibility approved must be consolidated in some type of Cost/Benefit Analysis for review and selection by the Steering Committee. As stated earlier, organizations should not be attempting to complete all projects at once, so selection of projects that align best with the organization's operational strategy would normally be selected first. Although, based on the organization's Safety, Quality, Delivery, and Cost main pains, the Steering Committee may select other projects as a priority. An example of a Cost/Benefit scoring matrix is shown below.

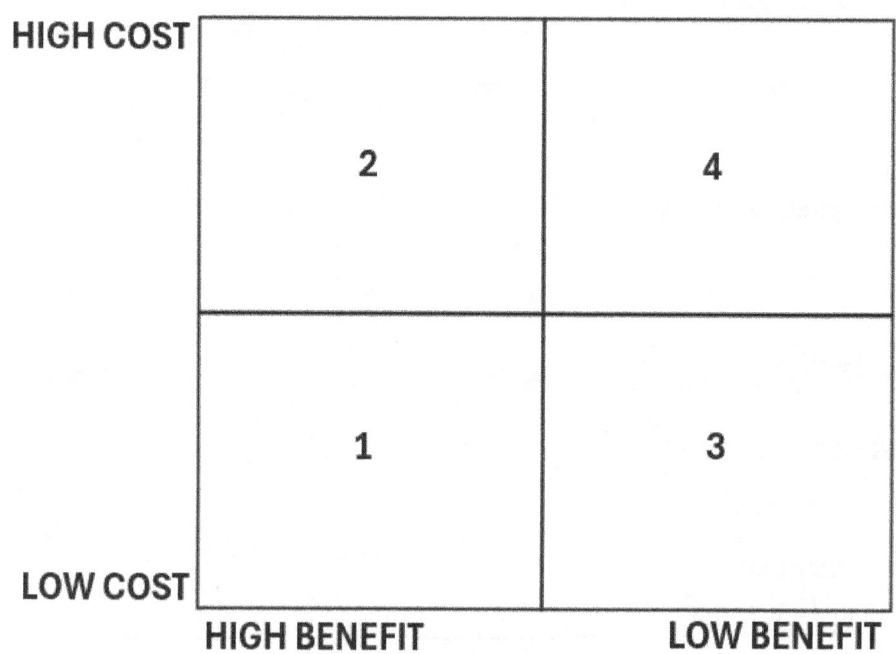

Site Improvement Projects Management Review.

Prior to review by the Site Improvement Steering Committee, all proposed new projects should have completed the Feasibility and Cost/Benefit analysis and be arranged in Cost/Benefit scoring order for presentation. Ongoing projects should have been periodically reviewed by the project's leaders and their managers for compliance with the original project plan timing and savings projection prior to presentation to the Steering Committee. Projects that have an unfavorable gap to goal should have adequate countermeasure actions to recover the project to compliance status. Projects that project savings in excess of the original project plans should be favorably adjusted on the Site Improvement Plan. The Site Improvement Plan's accuracy should be constantly maintained.

It is important to have adequate top echelon management support in the Steering Committee review to assure adequate resource support for ongoing and new projects. Ongoing projects countermeasure actions and resource issues should have already been resolved in prior management reviews so that the Steering Committee has accurate projects status.

Projects status presented by projects leaders in management review and to the Steering Committee should be clear and concise, showing actual progress against the original project schedule. A Gantt Chart format or other project status format should be used to accurately plan and present. A Gantt Schedule example is shown below.

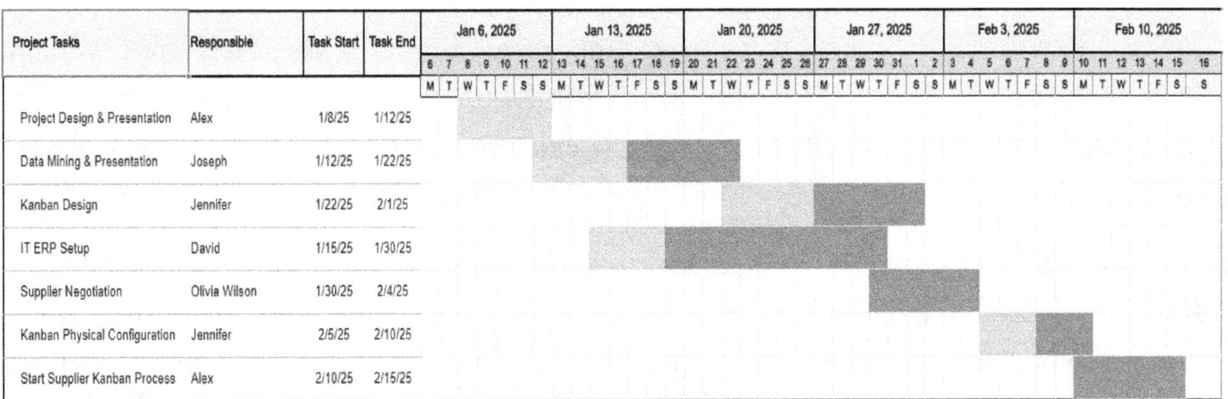

Project Tasks	Responsible	Task Start	Task End
Project Design & Presentation	Alex	1/8/25	1/12/25
Data Mining & Presentation	Joseph	1/12/25	1/22/25
Kanban Design	Jennifer	1/22/25	2/1/25
IT ERP Setup	David	1/15/25	1/30/25
Supplier Negotiation	Olivia Wilson	1/30/25	2/4/25
Kanban Physical Configuration	Jennifer	2/5/25	2/10/25
Start Supplier Kanban Process	Alex	2/10/25	2/15/25

The Site Improvement Planning Steering Committee.

The Site Improvement Steering Committee should ideally consist of personnel with Site Management responsibility and direct departmental Profit & Loss responsibility, to include the organization's Site Leader, Finance, Operations, Supply Chain, and other subject matter experts. It is very important that the Site Improvement Steering Committee has all required information available during the Site Improvement Planning reviews. This information will aid the committee in selecting the appropriate waste/cost reduction projects to ensure compliance with the organization's Financial and Strategic budgeted goals.

A summary report of the current year-to-date status against strategy goals is recommended, to include:

- Year-to-Date actual achieved savings versus budgeted savings, to include favorable or unfavorable gap analysis.
- Forward Year Remaining Site Improvement Plan projected savings versus Year Remaining budgeted savings.
- Year-to-Date Profit & Loss Statement Gap Analysis. This will be used to determine if additional projects are necessary to comply with projected budgeted savings.
- A summary list of ongoing and proposed projects by description, projected savings, and Cost/Benefit rating
- The Current State Projects Resource Allocation Summary.

Site Improvement Plan Resources Allocation

Project Resources Planning is another important factor in the Site Improvement Planning process. If resource allocation is a bottleneck to selecting high priority projects, then valuable priority projects may be delayed, or resources allocation will have to be modified.

An abbreviated example of an Excel multiple projects allocation matrix is shown below. It can be created to have "drop down" selection or "pivot table" selection. Also, can be created to be presented as a "RACI" (Responsible, Accountable, Consulted, Informed) type resource allocation format.

PROJECT NAME/NUMBER	PROJECT DATES	SPONSOR	LEADER	FINANCE	TECHNICAL 1	TECHNICAL 2	TECHNICAL 3	TECHNICAL 4
Kaizen-Assembly Flow	1/1/25-1/10/25	John	Laura	Zack	Allie	Gillian	Victor	Lynn
Kaizen-Kanban Pull Plating	1/6/25-1/15/25	John	Jim	Larry	Betsy	Joe	Vicky	Ingrid
Sourcing Negotiation XYZ	1/8/25-2/15/25	Sidney	Alex	Zack	Joseph	Jenifer	David	

The Visible Resource Allocation matrix can be used for multiple purposes:

- To ensure that projects have adequate resources to successfully complete the project.
- A visible format that can be quickly modified for projects resource allocation changes if necessary.
- An information communication tool to inform organization managers, supervisors, and associates regarding their schedule of project participation.
- An input record to the organizations' Lean Training Matrix. The Lean Training Matrix can also be an input to the Projects Resource Allocation Matrix for selection of personnel based on projects skill set requirements.

Aligning Strategic, Financial and Operational Indicators

Once the Steering Committee has made selection additions and modifications to the Site Improvement Plan, and projects resource allocation is complete, and the projects are officially scheduled, the Revised Site Improvement Plan should be reconciled again with the financial and strategy schedules below.

- Current month Profit & Loss budget to ensure projects savings are on track to achieve the projected Profit & Loss.
- Current 12 months rolling forward budget to ensure that the Site Improvement Plan has sufficient project savings to achieve the budget.
- Current Strategy Planning for reconciliation with Strategy metrics.

The reconciliation process should ensure that the most recent Site Improvement Plan meets or exceeds the organization's financial Profit & Loss, Budget requirements, and Strategy Planning requirements. If financial or strategy planning gaps are discovered, the organization must apply countermeasure actions to close the gaps. This may require specific projects countermeasure actions or submitting additional projects to the Site Improvement Planning process.

The Site Improvement Planning process requires constant managerial due diligence. It's importance as a Lean Business System cultural change enabler cannot be overstated.

Burn the Boats - Enjoy the Journey

UNIT 5 - STRATEGY TOOLS & CULTURE

Strategy Planning, Deployment, and Achievement

Arriving at the Strategy Tools & Culture unit, one might wonder why this unit is the last of the five Lean Business System Tools and Culture units. As the Lean Business System process gains traction, there is really no beginning or end. Granted, the system does require rigorous management oversight, but as each of the cultural phases gains momentum, the process transitions exponentially into a seamless self-perpetuating continuous improvement machine. The Lean Business System becomes a DNA component of the organization, driven by the organization's Mission, Vision, and Values.

The Strategy Tools and Culture building block employs Strategy Planning Methodology to develop stakeholder focused organizational strategic direction. The Strategy Planning Methodology is designed to develop:

- Specific top level strategic direction for the organization.
- Specific top level Lagging Key Performance Indicators measurement.
- Cascading departmental action plans to achieve the top level strategy.
- Cascading departmental Leading Performance Indicators measurement.
- Cascading departmental action plans to achieve the Leading Performance Indicators.
- Daily Management (NOW indicators) to assure compliance to both Lagging and Leading Performance Indicators.
- A frequent periodic Top Echelon Management review process.

Depending on the size and/or complexity of the business, Strategy Planning may be based on several inputs, to include:

- Current Business State across all business disciplines.
- Corporate Initiatives.
- Market & competitor influences.
- Stakeholder's concerns (Customers, Associates, Shareholders, Community).
- Current and forecasted economic influences.
- Government regulations.

- Technology advances.

The Value Driver Tree

The Value Driver Tree can be used as a Kaizen Culture Tool, a Financial Culture Tool, and a Strategy Culture Tool. Since the input detail for the Profit & Loss (Income Statement) can be lengthy and complex for some organizations, the Value Driver Tree can aid to identify key areas that drive either positive or negative impact for the organization.

- As a Kaizen Culture Tool: The Value Driver Tree can aid Profit & Loss accountable managers and continuous improvement personnel to identify specific areas of improvement opportunities.
- As a Financial Culture Tool: The Value Driver Tree as a Kaizen Culture Tool is significant, but also in the budgetary planning process, ensuring that key value drivers are addressed.
- As a Strategy Culture Tool: The Value Driver Tree is a Strategy Planning preparation tool to aid management in focusing on Key Value Drivers associated with Stakeholder's requirements.

An example of a Value Driver Tree is shown below. This abbreviated example identifies drivers for Profit & Loss Gross Profit, but can be utilized for any situation where key value decision drivers require identification. The items identified with a $ would include the currency value for each category. This tool can be used for other organizational non-currency initiatives, such as Customer Satisfaction or Employee Satisfaction.

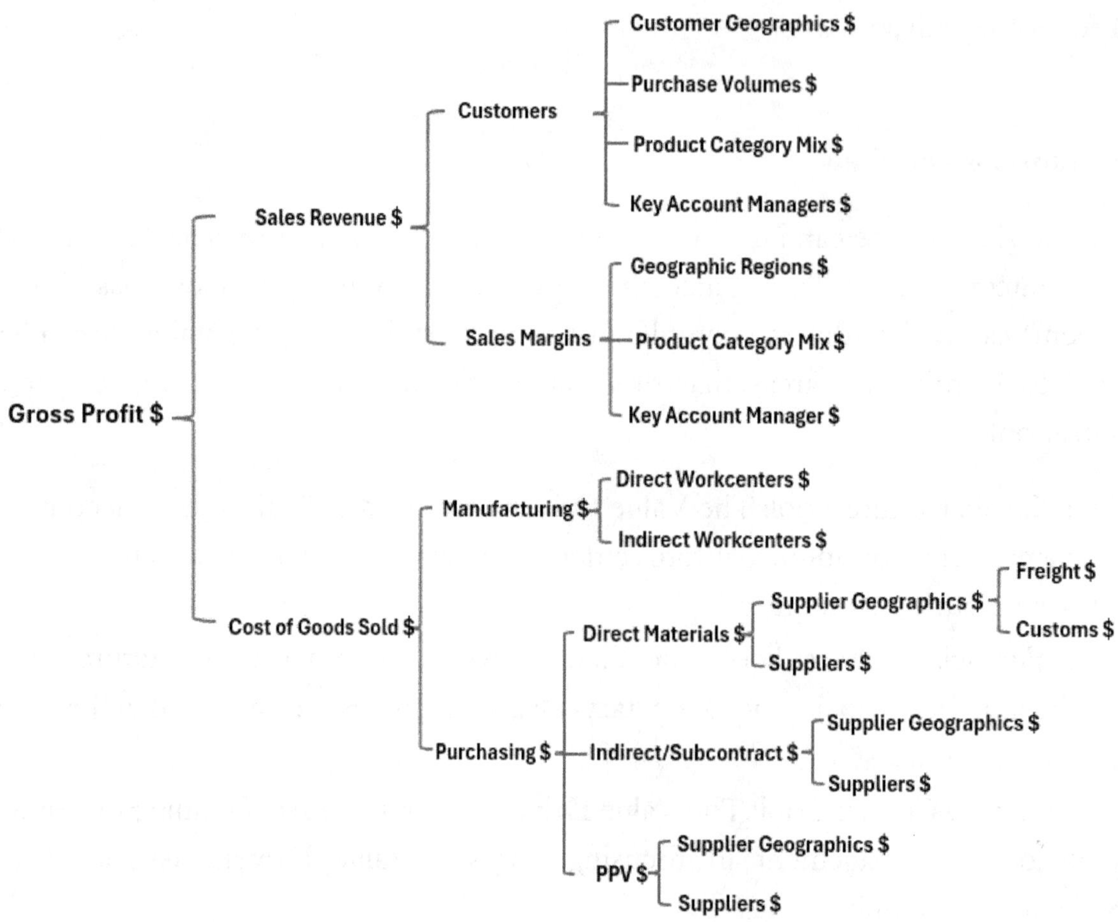

Hoshin Kanri Methodology

There are several different Strategy Planning Methodologies and formats to select from when performing the Strategy Planning exercise. The planning methodology selection will normally depend on the size and/or complexity of the organization. For example, for a business just starting out, their Mission, Vision, Values, and Strategy Planning might be on a one page note pad. But what is important to note is that any type of Strategy Planning is not a one person task unless the organization is a one person organization. Even then, the help from an experienced outside business advisor may be very helpful.

For the purpose of the Strategy Tools and Culture Building Block, the Hoshin Kanri Methodology and format will be used. This is also referred to as the "X Matrix".

Some of the advantages of using the Hoshin Kanri Methodology and X Matrix Format are:

- Requires engagement from key organizational management resources.
- Aids the organization to focus on both long term and short term organizational needs.
- Aligns the organization to common priorities through cascading objectives.
- Provides objectives achievement planning, tracking and countermeasures.
- Works well as a consistent communication tool for all organizational stakeholders.

An abbreviated example of the Hoshin Kanri (X Matrix) Strategy Planning format is shown below.

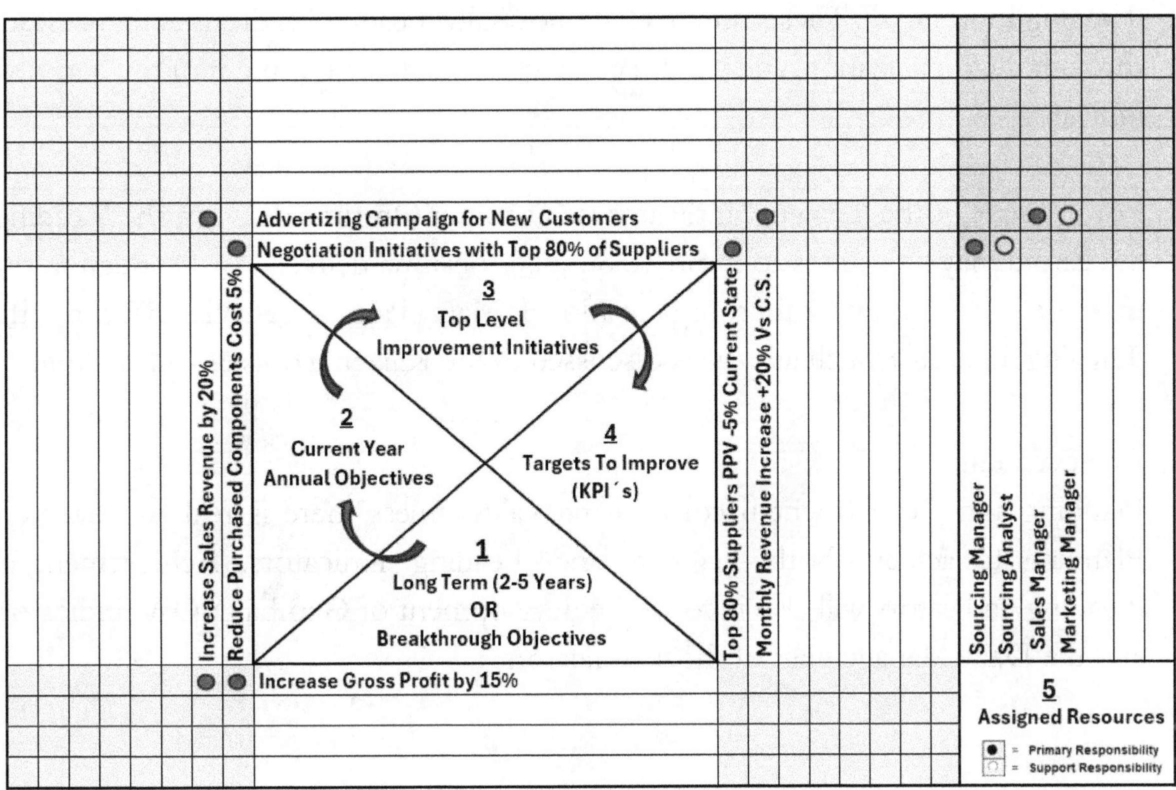

Strategy Planning, Deployment, & Achievement Process

As mentioned above, an organization's size and complexity may guide the organization to the appropriate Strategy Planning process, but it is paramount that cascading objectives deployment and achievement planning are included in the process. An example of a Strategy Planning Process is shown below. The example includes three important phases:

- Planning
  Development of the organization's strategy to meet or exceed stakeholder's business expectations. These are normally 'Lagging' Business Key Performance Indicators

- Deployment:
  The planning and development of initiatives to achieve the Strategy Planning 'Lagging Indicators". These initiatives are normally 'Leading' Indicators that cascade through the organization, and will focus specifically on achievement of the 'Lagging' indicator.

  For example, if the 'Lagging' Indicator is Customer On-time delivery, the 'Leading' indicators may be actions to improve Supplier on-time delivery, or Production on-time delivery, or any other organizational Main Pain negatively affecting the 'Lagging' indicator, such as wastes discussed in the Kaizen Tools & Culture unit.

- Achievement:
  Planning and Deployment become of no value unless there is real Achievement Planning to achieve both 'Lagging' and 'Leading' indicators. Achievement of 'Leading' indicators will also involve the development of Gemba 'NOW' indicators and the Daily Management of those indicators.

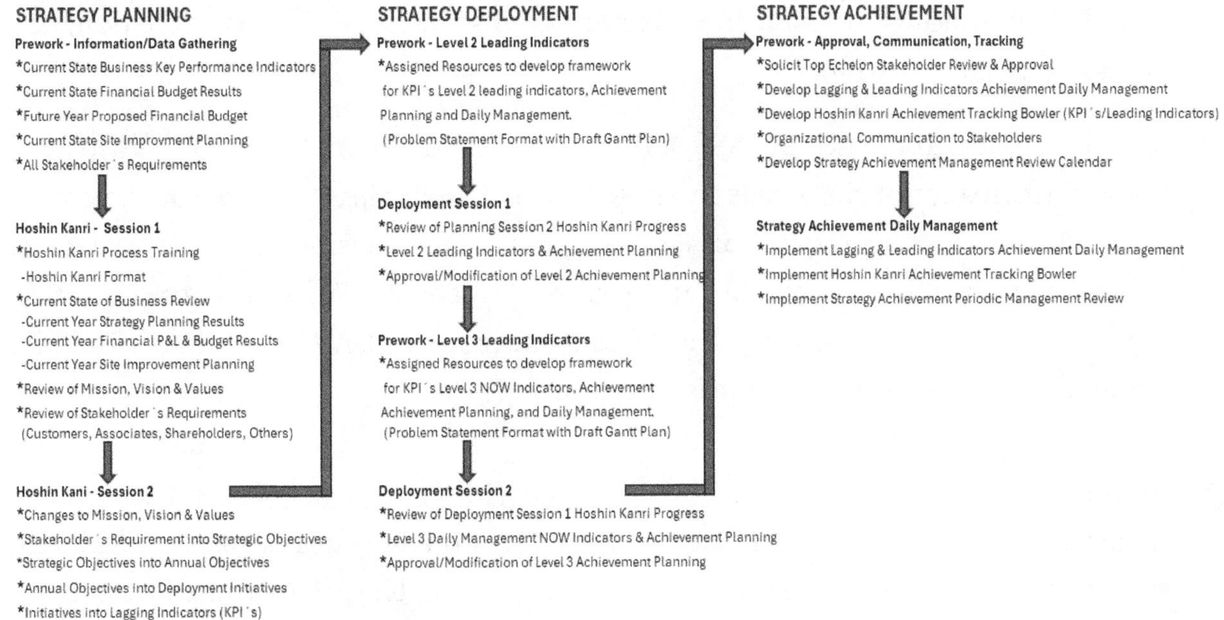

Strategy Achievement Sustainability

One of the important process components in the above Strategy Planning process is the Hoshin Kanri Achievement Planning Tracking Bowler. After development and approval of the Strategy Planning and Deployment phases, an achievement tracking and reporting tool is required to ensure that lagging Key Performance Indicators and leading Performance Indicators are yielding the planned results.

An abbreviated example of an Excel Strategy Planning Bowler Tracking Tool is shown below for reference.

COMPANY ABCXYZ STRATEGY PLANNING BOWLER EXAMPLE

Breakthrough Objective	Current Year Objective	Current Year KPI´s	Responsible	Plan/Actua	Jan	Feb	Mar	YTD Resuts
Increase Operating Profit	Increase Sales Revenue $1M	Monthly Sales Increase $83,400	Sales Mgr	PLANNED	$83,400	$83,400	$83,400	$250,200
				ACTUAL	$70,000	$75,000	$85,000	$230,000
Increase Operating Profit	Reduce Purchased Cost $500K	Monthly Favorable PPV $42,000	Sourcing Mgr	PLANNED	$42,000	$42,000	$42,000	$126,000
				ACTUAL	40,000	45,000	45,000	$130,000

The above example shows two year-to-date Key Performance Indicators extracted from the Hoshin Kanri Strategy Planning Tool being tracked by the Strategy Planning

Bowler. The two shown metrics are an extraction of several metrics that were designed to increase Operating Profit.

- Monthly Sales Increase of $83,400: January and February results displayed underperformance of the achievement planning, which meant that the achievement planning was too aggressive or lacked appropriate decision data. In this case, countermeasure actions would be required to comply with the original Key Performance Indicator, and the modified achievement plan Gantt Chart would be updated to reflect the countermeasure actions.

- Monthly Favorable Purchase Price Variance (PPV) of $42,000: January results underperformed, but countermeasure actions had traction in February and March, and now the results are exceeding the year-to-date Key Performance Indicator amount of $126,000.

As important as Strategy is to achieve the Vision and Mission of the organization, and to satisfy changing stakeholder's expectations, strategy planning has little value if the other Lean Business System tools and cultures are lacking. Just imagine Strategy Planning, Strategy Deployment, and Achievement Execution with poor management engagement, unstable Gemba practices, unsustainable Kaizen improvements, and inadequate Financial engagement and alignment.

UNIT 6 – LEAN BUSINESS SYSTEM IMPLEMENTATION & SUSTAINABILITY

Project Management, Associate Engagement, and Management Review

At the severe risk of being repetitive, it is worth mentioning again that the Lean Business System implementation and sustainability progress is dependent on Consistent Management Engagement and Dedication to the process, as discussed in the Introduction.

Project Management oversight and accountability is required for a successful implementation. Whether Project Management is dedicated or not depends on the size, complexity, and current Lean Business System maturity of an organization. But either way, the suggestion is to develop a project managed implementation schedule with Gantt type implementation planning and execution. It is important to implement all of the topics reviewed in the five Lean Business System Building Blocks. An organization can include additional items as desired, but it is highly recommended to not pass over any topics, even as simple as they may seem to organizational management.

Specific Lean Business System tasks accountability is required throughout all of the five building blocks. There is an old Portuguese adage that translated recites: ***"A dog with two owners starves to death".*** The Project Management warning in the message is to not get caught in the multiple owner's responsibility pitfalls, leading to finger pointing, during either the building blocks implementation phases, or the continuous improvement sustainability phases.

Lean Business System Implementation Checklist

An example checklist of the Lean Business System topics covered is shown below, and can be used to develop the implementation plan. The Codes placed in the weeks column is an example of how the project management scheduling tool can be used.

MANAGEMENT TOOLS & CULTURE		MONTH 1					MONTH 2				MONTH 3			
Code	**Lean Business System Tasks**	WK 01	WK 02	WK 03	WK 04	WK 05	WK 06	WK 07	WK 08	WK 09	WK 10	WK 11	WK 12	WK 13
M01	Lean Business System Overview	M01												
M02	Management Approval to Proceed	M02												
M03	Assessment Current State Lean Business Process		M03	M03										
M04	Lean Tools & Cultures				M04									
M05	Supporting Management Hiearchy				M05									
M06	Toyota Production System Alignment				M06									
M07	Leader Standard Work					M07								
M08	Associate Training Design					M08								
M09	Safety, Quality, Delivery, Cost Compas					M09								
M10	Associate Engagement/Associate Satisfaction					M10								
M11	Management Mindset-Failure is not an Option					M11								

GEMBA TOOLS & CULTURE		MONTH 1					MONTH 2				MONTH 3			
Code	**Lean Business System Tasks**	WK 01	WK 02	WK 03	WK 04	WK 05	WK 06	WK 07	WK 08	WK 09	WK 10	WK 11	WK 12	WK 13
G01	Gemba Methodology													
G02	Gemba Stabilization-Safety, Quality, Delivery, Cost													
G03	Value Add Versus Non-Value Add													
G04	The 9 Wastes													
G05	5S & 6S													
G06	Visual Management, Lagging-Leading-Now Indicators													
G07	Tier Level Safety, Quality, Delivery, Cost Management													
G08	Escalation & Accountability													
G09	Rapid Response Board													
G10	Responsibility Boad													
G11	Operational Standards													
G12	Plan-Do-Act/Adjust-Check													
G13	Problem Solving, 5 Whys, Ishikawa Methodologies													
G14	Associate Training - Skills Matrix													
G15	Process and Product Quality In Gemba Culture													
G16	Gemba Sense of Urgency													
G17	Associate Respect, Engagement & Empowerment													
G18	Burn The Boats - Is Everybody In?													

KAIZEN TOOLS & CULTURE		MONTH 1					MONTH 2				MONTH 3			
K01	What is Kaizen Training													
K02	Review of Lean Tools Roadmap													
K03	COPQ, Effect on P&L, COPQ Improvements													
K04	Gemba Waste Reduction-Are Results Being Realized?													
K05	Employees Indeas Program													
K06	Profit & Loss (Income Statement) Variations Review													
K07	Value Stream Mapping (VSM)													
K08	Design For Flow Methodology													
K09	Mateials Flow-Warehouse, Supermarkets, Point of Use													
K10	Production Planning Level Loading													
K11	Production Planning Set-up Wheel													
K12	Overall Equipment Effectiveness - The Metric, The Tool													
K13	Single Minute Exchange of Dies (SMED)													
K14	Total Productive Maintenance, Preventative, Autonomous													
K15	Value Analysis/Value Engineering (VA/VE)													
K16	Material Pull Systems-Pull, Push, Hybrid													
K17	Engergy Kaizen, Carbon Footprint Reduction													
K18	Materials Management Support of Kaizen Culture													
K19	Kaizen Events													
K20	Pursuit of Perfection Mindset													
K21	Burn The Boats - Is Everybody In?													

FINANCIAL TOOLS & CULTURE		MONTH 1				MONTH 2				MONTH 3			
F01	Profit & Loss Overview-Use Organization´s P&L												
F02	Increasing Cost, Pricing & Profit												
F03	Key Financial Indicators-Root Cause & Countermeasures												
F04	Site Improvement Planning Process												
F05	Site Improvement Planning Tool												
F06	Projects Feasibility Review												
F07	Cost/Benefit Review-Four Quad Format												
F08	Site Improvement Planning Management Review												
F09	Site Improvement Planning Steering Committee												
F10	Site Improvement Planning Resources Allocation												
F11	Aligning Strategic, Financial, and Operational Indicators												
F12	Burn The Boats - Is Everybody In?												

STRATEGY TOOLS & CULTURE		MONTH 1				MONTH 2				MONTH 3			
S01	What is Strategy Planning, Deployment & Achievement												
S02	The Value Driver Tree												
S03	What Strategy Planning to Use-Hoshin Kanri Methodology												
S04	Strategy Planning, Deployment & Achievement Process												
S05	Strategy Achievement Sustainability												
S06	Successful Implementation & Sustainability Accountability												
S07	Associate Engagement & Satisfaction Swimlane Format												
S08	Mission, Vision & Values Drives The Lean Business System												

Associates Engagement/Satisfaction Swimlanes Format

Below is the Associate Engagement/Satisfaction Swimlane format example that was covered in the Management Tools & Culture Unit. As discussed earlier, there is a difference between Associate Engagement and Associate Satisfaction. It is important to understand the difference when designing the Associate focused Engagement & Satisfaction Planning. The planning tool should be used hand-in-hand with the Lean Business System implementation & sustainability tool.

Lean Business System IMPLEMENTATION CULTURAL SWIM LANES (example)

TOOLS & CULTURES	JANUARY	FEBRUARY	MARCH	APRIL	MAY	JUNE
MANAGEMENT						
GEMBA						
KAIZEN						
FINANCIAL						
STRATEGY						

Lean tools alone, no matter how well they are executed, will not suffice for the whole Lean Business System. Developing highly engaged, highly satisfied, and high performance associates are the other addends of the Lean Business System sum equation.

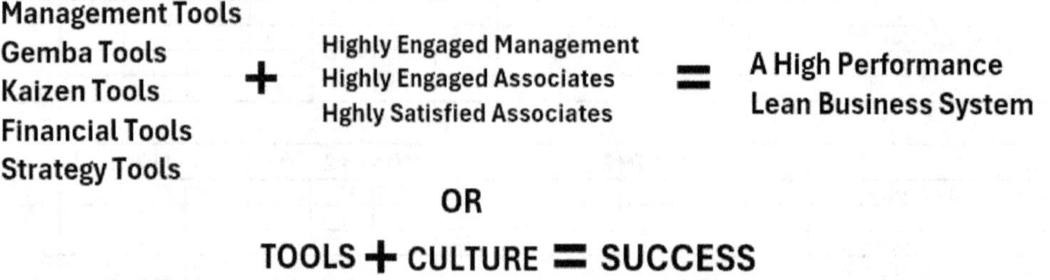

Conclusion

The Lean Business System journey is a professional lifelong endeavor not to be taken lightly. But when correctly implemented, and sustained, everyone in the organization develops a professional life that evolves toward a greatly more satisfying and rewarding endeavor.

The Lean Business System, driven by the organizations' Mission, Vision, and Values utilizes the five building blocks tools to create a sustainable continuous improvement Business System with year-over-year exponentially improving results, fueled by culturally empowered high performance associates. A self-perpetuating business cash machine that performs better-and-better, year-over-year.

Burn the Boats - Enjoy the Journey

www.ingramcontent.com/pod-product-compliance
Lightning Source LLC
Chambersburg PA
CBHW051337200326
41519CB00026B/7461

* 9 7 9 8 9 9 2 7 6 1 4 7 4 *